A COLLECTION OF THOUGHTS

VOLUME 1:

THE MYSTERY OF LOVE

Ricky J. Nutt

A Collection of Thoughts Volume 1: The Mystery of Love

Copyright © 2011 by R.J. Nutt

Originally published as *A Collection of Thoughts on the Mystery of Love* © 2009

All rights reserved. No part of this book may be reproduced in any form without permission in writing from the publisher, except in the case of brief quotations embodied in critical articles or reviews.

Published by R.J. Nutt
Edited by Michele Lamons

Cover Design: www.royaltyvision.com
Cover Photo: Stephen Coburn
Back Cover Photo: Devin Dobson

A special thank you goes to Evergreen Printing in Vallejo, Ca. for their time and assistance.

Scripture taken from the HOLY BIBLE, NEW INTERNATIONAL VERSION. Copyright 1973, 1978, 1984 by International Bible Society. Used by permission of Zondervan. All rights reserved.

ISBN: 0-6155-0716-6
ISBN-13: 978-0-6155-0716-3

For more information about the author or for other inquiries visit:

www.rickyj330.com

Dedications

I would first like to thank my parents, Ricky and Veronica, for passing on to me a wonderful legacy of godliness, love, and faithfulness that I will never forget. Truly, God determines the times set for us and the exact places we should live. When I think of the parents I was given to watch over me and to train me up in righteousness, I cannot deny that I am divinely blessed. I love you both so much, and I thank you for all that you have poured into my life. My heart overflows with gratitude, for God giving me to you.

To my wife, Genevieve, I would like to say thank you also. Your encouragement, support, and love through the final years of this process have been a gift from Heaven. To be sure, God sent me the woman I needed, and I am overwhelmed by the grace God has shown me through you. I love you, and I hope that we can pass on to our children a legacy of love and faith that will encourage them to chase after the Glory we ourselves have seen.

To the rest of my family, I am honored to have you in my life. Your support and encouragement have not been overlooked. Do not neglect your gifts, but fan into flame what God has placed inside of you, and use them for the glory of the Master.

To my King,

"May the words of my mouth and the meditation of my heart be pleasing in your sight, O Lord, my Rock and Redeemer." Psalm 19:14

"We move through a world of mystery; and the deepest question is, what is the being that is ever near, sometimes felt, never seen — That which has haunted us from childhood with a dream of something surpassingly fair, which has never yet been realized — That which sweeps through the soul at times as a desolation, like the blast from the wings of the Angel of Death, leaving us stricken and silent in our loneliness — That which has touched us in our tenderest point, and the flesh has quivered with agony, and our mortal affections have shrivelled up with pain — That which comes to us in aspirations of nobleness, and conceptions of superhuman excellence.

Shall we say It or He? What is It? Who is He? Those anticipations of Immortality and God — what are they? Are they the mere throbbings of my own heart, heard and mistaken for a living something beside me? Are they the sound of my own wishes, echoing through the vast void of Nothingness? Or shall I call them God, Father, Spirit, Love? A living Being within me or outside me? Tell me Thy Name, thou awful mystery of Loveliness! This is the struggle of all earnest life."

F.W. Robertson, excerpt from "Jacob's Wrestling." (*Ten Sermons*)
June 10, 1849

CONTENTS

Preface

The End of Desire 21

They Shall See God 33

Deep and Hidden Things 41

A Horrible Misunderstanding 49

His Treasured Possession 63

The Light Was Good 71

Trustworthy and True 77

My People 91

All Things Exist for Him 109

I Was Not Aware 119

Your Voice is Sweet 129

Because I am Holy 139

No One Will See the Lord 149

Precious and Fine Pearls 161

PREFACE

Even today I am tired and weary, and I have walked a road that not many others have chosen to travel. I felt the call to live my life in a stranger way than most, and the passion that was in me, birthed by the Divine, took me down lonely and difficult roads. It led me toward a future that I could not see, and it showed me a path where bravery and boldness could not follow. And when those courageous friends abandoned me, it was Faith that held my hand to take me to a place I had hungered for so long to see.

As I write, I sit here wondering if anyone will ever hear these words of mine, knowing that others have gone through the same pain for a joy that has been set before them also. In my heart, though, Faith's confident voice continues to speak, reminding me of the promises that were made to me by Master so long ago. Like those before me, I am forced to wait for Him to fulfill His promise. I cannot change His timing; I must learn to set my watch to His.

I do not particularly mind being honest about the difficulty I faced, because I know that my authenticity will strike a chord within the hearts of those who read and who are thinking of one day traveling down the same road. I can recall periods of time when I could not even bring myself to write because of the disappointment and inadequacy I had felt time and time again. In each storm, however, there rested within my heart the hope of a bright and shining day, when His grace would tell me that the moment He promised was here, and that the crop I was tending had begun to bear fruit that I could share with the world.

As you read this work, then, understand that it was not without pain that its words were cultivated and prepared for the harvest. Know also, that what you will find here was not done for the sake of personal gain, but I labored for many years to complete this exposition for the sake of love, and today I share the fruits of my labor with you.

There were definitely moments when I regretted my decision, moments when I wondered why I could not have chosen the simple road. Then the Scriptures spoke to my heart by reminding me that even "if we are faithless, he will remain faithful, for he cannot disown himself,"[1] and I persevered toward His calling. As difficult as the journey's been, then, I am glad I chose to walk it. While I am sure its difficulty will increase dramatically as I am moved towards new horizons, I understand that at the end of the matter, there is an unparalleled Blessing I will enjoy. As I walk where He has called me to walk and complete the tasks that lay ahead, I will experience God's presence and love more fully in my heart and in my life.

It has taken me almost three years to figure out what would be the focus of this book, and over five interminable years spent laboring through changes and growth to finally cultivate something that could possibly bear fruit. To be sure, at the heart of the message was always to be an emphasis on the beauty and the glory of the divine love, but when I began the project, I think my excitement overshadowed the impending difficulty of the task; as time progressed, I was not sure how I would bring all of my thoughts together into a coherent piece.

I learned a lot from that uncomfortable frustration, but perhaps the most important epiphany came when I realized that the divine love is mysterious. It was this mystery that caused me many of the problems I had in pulling my thoughts and ideas together. Instead of despising that mystery, though, I embraced it, realizing that the mystery of love is one of its most remarkable characteristics. I realized that if the divine love could be fully comprehended, it could not be divine at all, and this vision of love transformed my writing into something far beyond my expectations.

To paint the picture of the revelation that came to me, I will use an illustration from nature. Perhaps the most mysterious part of our planet is the ocean, and this mystery stretches across the globe. The ocean holds tender and quiet secrets, wonders and beauties we have never even witnessed. What we see on the surface of these great waters of the earth is always a stirring image. The sun shimmers off the waves of the smooth liquid. Animals call this beauty their home. They rest, play and feed there, and sometimes we are able to watch.

While those waters are a remarkable and awe-inspiring creation, what we can perceive as we see them from the surface is only an obscure, albeit lovely, view of the true nature, depth, and span of those waters. Its deepest truth is hidden from mankind beneath layers of beautiful darkness, and God has made it that way. Since the beginning of time, man has looked out upon the ocean and seen terror and beauty, danger and glory. This intrigue will never wane, because the ocean is a fascinating picture of mystery and that mystery will forever titillate the curiosity of man. In that respect, it is an image of the Divine.

The geological record suggests that in the earth's younger years, the continents were all united as one immense land mass, surrounded by water on all sides. I am inclined to think that God did that intentionally as if to say, "The earth is here, but my mystery and my glory and my love surround it." No matter the shape that the earth takes, God's love will always surround His people. The continents may diverge, and its people's hearts might move further and further away from a concern for one another, but His love remains around us as a constant and unending presence.

Indeed, the ocean is mysterious and its mystery reminds us of the Divine. What we can perceive with the eyes of our imperfect hearts, as we take our glances at the heart of God, is only an obscure image of the surpassing glory that waits to be revealed to us. We certainly see an unmatched beauty when we look upon this great love with the eyes of our hearts open to wonder, but from where we stand in respect to that divine love, we can see only a precious piece: what lies beyond the horizon and what rests beneath the depths we cannot behold. What we see, though, is enough to inspire our imaginations and to stimulate our spiritual longings—to keep us wondering what great beauty remains hidden from our eyes that we may one day, if we persevere, be blessed to see.

There is precious and unique life beneath the surface of that beautiful mystery. A particularly strong and intense light can reveal it, but it is there, in the darkness, waiting for the light to shine.

We may one day find ourselves standing on the shore of time, looking upon the waters of love, being captivated by the images it forces our hearts to contemplate. When we finally choose to dive beneath the surface to explore that Divine Mystery, what lies there in that dim darkness becomes clearer as the Great Light begins to shine in our hearts. And the more time we spend there, exploring the mystery, the more beauty we will enjoy.

With eagerness and expectation I embraced love's mystery. I was eager to study, and I was excited about the prospect that the work of my feeble hands and my simple mind might help others realize one eternal truth: God's heart is bound to mankind by virtue of a love we cannot comprehend. After much time had passed, I finally came to the relieving conclusion that it was not so much necessary or even possible for me to provide a perfect description of that transcendent love that binds us to the heart of God. As one writer so aptly explained "mystery has beauty and power, only as we seek to penetrate it, as we see its far-reaching implications, as it overpowers and engulfs us."[2] Therefore, I wrote about God's transcendent love "not so much to explain it as to allow its depth and its beauty to inspire...."[3] What was produced, as a result, was this collection of thoughts.

Now, if there is one thing we must understand before we approach the subject of divine love it is this: "love comes from God." I cannot talk about the divine affection without discussing the Grace from whom it proceeds. To do so would cause more confusion than it would convey spiritual truth. The grandeur and the glory of the Holy One took me on a journey of heart and soul. As I traveled and studied on that wonderful sea of mystery, my thoughts became broader and more comprehensive. For this reason, this collection of thoughts not only discusses the holy nature of the divine love, but in my thoughts the reader might see visions of who our God of love truly is, what He does because of His love for us, and what the existence of that love should mean to us all. This is a book about human spirituality and our relation to the Divine.

I am confident the ultimate direction in which it will point you will be Heavenward and nowhere else, toward a *true* and *living way* opened for us by God Himself. There, in the heart of God, will you find all the solace and the satisfaction you will ever need in life.

Within this collection of thoughts, you will find ideas pointing to God's holiness, references to light, and visions of fire (among many other things) referred to and repeated throughout. This was not done intentionally on my part, and only in the latter stages did it become an issue with which I felt the need to address. As I continued my studies, these truths kept coming to the forefront, and the thoughts I felt so important, they must be reiterated. In places where ideas are repeated, I feel I explain their presence well enough to make obvious their relevance to that chapter, but as I realized the present issue, I saw how these recurring ideas function as a sort of linguistic ligament that connect my thoughts to one another.

Indeed, the splendor of God's love has many shades, but those radiant colors all coalesce in the harmony of Divinity to create within our hearts a single, unified image of pure and unapproachable light that is the glory of the King eternal, immortal, invisible.

You may also notice a number of allusions to natural images, and many analogies developed from the same ilk. One of the servants of Jesus Christ tells us in Romans that "since the creation of the world God's invisible qualities—his eternal power and divine nature—have been clearly seen, being understood from what has been made…"[4] Now, nature is certainly not the measuring rod for spiritual revelation, but I do wholeheartedly agree with the old preacher's words: "All earthly things are the shadows of heavenly realities—the expression, in created, visible forms, of the invisible glory of God."[5] So while I enjoy God's creation with reverent curiosity, I am often lost in moments of reflection and contemplation and find definite parallels between spiritual truths learned in Scripture and the expression of God's beautiful creation.

While the fullness of God's visible creation is extraordinarily beautiful, the moment He formed mankind was "the climax, the glory, and the crown" of all His mighty works.[6] According to the Holy Scriptures, mankind was made "in the image of God."[7] That is not to say that man shares in the prerogatives or the powers of Divinity, neither does it attribute the nature of God to man, but it does suggest that spiritually, God and man, share a common connection. In the beginning, God "breathed into [man's] nostrils the breath of life," animating him, and transforming the dust and clay from which he was formed, into "a living being."[8] If man were an article of clothing, then God would be the thread that holds him together. He gives us an identity, a form, and a purpose. Not that He abides as an indwelling presence in *all* things, and has fellowship with *everyone*, but truly, He "created all things, and by [His] will they were created and have their being."[9]

Our God-given spiritual nature provides the possibility for us to know our Maker in marvelous manifestation and to commune with our Creator in constant love. That potential, though, should not be misunderstood as an infinite and unbroken communion with all things. Certainly, God wants to know us all, and at the beginning of creation, man was made to experience the glories of the Divine. Unfortunately, we are painfully separated from His presence, and we must learn what is needed for us to return to the Origin of Life, to find the happiness we have for so long been searching. Truly, God longs to captivate our hearts with His glory.

We are all divinely *designed* and divinely *desired*. Our spirituality will never be properly exercised, however, until we find Him for whom our spirits search, and learn to respond appropriately to His loving presence. God holds us together, as the Thread of Existence, just as He upholds all things. But we ought to desire more than just simple existence; we ought to be looking for genuine, spiritual life, which Adam tasted in the beginning, before he was deceived.

The most extraordinary experience of the human existence is enjoyed only in the heart of our Blessed Maker. His Son Jesus Christ defined this relationship with such brilliant clarity when He said, "Now this is eternal life: that they may know [The Father], the only true God...."[10] It is my hope, then, that through this piece some might touch the very heart of God and discover for themselves a revelation of our Heavenly Father's surpassingly great love, so that they might be "filled to the measure of all the fullness of God."[11] And continually seek after that most delightful and awe-inspiring Presence for which we were made to enjoy.

I am not a philosopher or a scholar. I am not a theologian or a pastor. I am a curious believer who has pursued the Great King for answers, who has approached His throne in reverent fear and bothered Him with love and adoration and attention, and He did not turn me away. He let me draw close and He answered my questions with patient and hopeful love. Therefore, I pray that the seekers of the world will benefit from the fruit of my curiosity.

Yet, as I consider the reality of my talent and my learning, my mind introduces me to the unfortunate possibility that perhaps none of my sentiments or thoughts about the mystery of love will ever be considered insightful or revealing statements on human spirituality and our connection to the Divine. This is only to be expected considering the mood of many today. I write out of the darkness, with no fame to speak of and no platform from which to promote myself as so many others do today, and I am sure this alone will keep me silent for some time. Indeed, it should not matter much to me whether or not I am praised or rejected for my efforts. I should write only for the sake of my conscience and my calling. I should write so that my Master will one day utter the words, "Well done good and faithful servant."[12] That is my glory, for Him to say that He is pleased.

Nevertheless, I think the thing that makes a book worth reading is an ability to touch the hearts of successive generations with words that inspire a positive and blessed change. The author should speak to the human and to the spirit, with words that give life and hope no matter the time or place in which the readers may find themselves. I hope that once any possible excitement wanes and time progresses, this book might, like kindling buried among the ashes, always maintain a remnant of fire that can be used to ignite a new flame in the hearts of those who need it.

After years of labor, I think the harvest is finally here, and to the world I offer only a collection of my thoughts, hoping it might inspire someone new to experience the presence of Majesty in their life. As I worked toward the conclusion of this piece, I was encouraged by the insightful words of the late A.W. Tozer:

> if we would know God and for other's sake tell what we know, we must try to speak of His love. All Christians have tried, but none has ever done it very well. I can no more do justice to that awesome and wonder-filled theme than a child can grasp a star. Still, by reaching toward the star the child may call attention to it and even indicate the direction one must look to see it. So, as I stretch my heart toward the high, shining love of God, someone who has not before known about it may be encouraged to look up and have hope.[13]

Understanding the sentiment of that great Christian thinker, I resolve to know that the words of any man or woman would not be able to sufficiently describe such a magnificent theme. I am content, and rather relieved, to know that His love for mankind cannot be reduced to a measurable and explicable emotion. Yet, it can be received by faith and welcomed into the hearts and the spirits of those who were made to enjoy its presence forever.

If by pointing to this great spiritual virtue, my words might contribute to the positive progress of some person, family, or relationship, I will be filled with an unspeakable joy to know that my obedience was not in vain. And so, like the frail child that I am, I stretch my mind and my heart toward the bright and shining love of God, to the undimmed heart of the King eternal, immortal, invisible—that all might find its direction and that someone might look to Him and have hope.

R.J. Nutt

A COLLECTION OF THOUGHTS

VOLUME 1:

THE MYSTERY OF LOVE

THE END OF DESIRE

Thoughts on the Sadness of the Human Condition and the Glorious Sufficiency of God

"As the deer pants for streams of water, so my soul pants for you, O God. My soul thirsts for God, for the living God. When can I go and meet with God?" Psalm 42:1-2

Our souls are thirsty, and no matter how hard we may try we cannot deny it; we are longing for something that can satisfy our often unquenchable desire. The pleasures of a wayward life can grant some semblance of satisfaction, but its scent is not sweet enough to deceive us completely, and eventually its intoxicating aroma turns stale. The uniform biblical message teaches us a particular truth: there is within us all, whether we can feel it in our souls or whether the quality of our lives reveal it to us naturally, a great lack of some sort. There is a sense of longing, a spiritual deficiency deep within us, which cannot be satisfied by anything our humanity can provide. As a result of this prodigious internal poverty, we are forced to begin a glorious and dangerous pursuit for something that can satisfy our desire.

To understand the matter, we should consider ourselves in a different light than we often do. We should see ourselves as a man stranded on a deserted island, hoping to come across some sign of intelligent life. Or if this does not begin to draw an image, let us consider ourselves as a journeyman who, after a very warm day traveling, is looking for water to ease the burning of the elements. And when that man finds water—an ocean perhaps—he looks upon that glorious savior with eyes of joy and for a moment, he soaks in the beauty of his new-found comforter. Yet, the man will not rest content to just watch the waters crash against the shore near him. No, the man after such a long journey, will run to those waters and take a dip to relieve his weariness, and in those waters he will be comforted. He might rest for a moment to enjoy its beauty and grace on a shore nearby in soft and cool sands, but if he has truly found what he was for so long searching, and if he wants to find comfort and have his soul rejuvenated, he must dare to dive into the waters. Just seeing the blessing is not enough, he must dip beneath the surface to enjoy its finer beauties.

If we took a survey of hearts, we might find that the overwhelming majority have marked as their loftiest desire "to love and to be loved forever." While we long for love above all else, we have been scorched by the heat of loneliness, and we have become convinced that only finding love can ease the pain we feel; this is the human condition. Instead of looking toward the heavenly love, though, we fix our eyes on those around us. Eventually, and this usually after much disappointment, we discover that even they are lacking what we truly desire; sadly, they cannot give us what we need.

We approach them with the same thirst. We fix our eyes on their waters, and each time we hurry toward them to dive into their love, our eyes open to the mirage. We expend all our heart's energy, only later to discover we are being deceived. Still, we continue to look around us, hoping one day someone will appear and gift us with what we so deeply desire. Unfortunately, they never come, and eventually we realize we have no clue where to look to cure our decrepit condition.

So we search and hope for fortuitous moments of opportunity, when chance might deliver the perfect mate into our arms. Our experiences with what we know of love have left us in a precarious position. We want satisfaction, but this very sad fact hangs darkly over our heads and hearts; we just do not know where we ought to look. If we could have seen the truth, we would have done things differently long before. We would have realized that the *human* cannot satisfy the *spirit*. What we desire, we have never experienced, and the hunger we have cannot be quenched via natural means. This unfruitful pursuit leads us to ask the question, "Where can a satisfying love be found?" If our lives are to change, if the desire of hearts is to be fulfilled, we must find the answer.

Most realize already that human love can only grant a glimmer of satisfaction. It is, in one respect, like a Chameleon, because its environment often compels a change in its appearance. It is not powerful enough to change its environment, and so, to protect itself, it will eventually change—it must always care for itself. When the dangers of the world sit ominously near, its affection will undoubtedly change to defend against possible hurt. However, taking a look at human love may give us insight into the divine. Human love comes from the soul of man, therefore, it is not simply a manifestation of biological impulses; its origins are more complex. We are not forced to love, but rather, we choose to love. This is why we say, "It comes from the heart," because we have the ability to withhold love and also the ability to give it.

In the same way, the supernal love for which we are searching has a "source"—a spring from which it flows to give life to thirsty hearts. This love is divine and mysterious in nature and emanation, but if we would like to say from where it comes, we would say "It comes from the heart *of God*." Truly, God is the source of all perfect love.[14] It flows from the Eternal One like water from a newfound spring, unending and pure, undefiled and incomparable. All who are brave enough to search it out and drink from its fountain realize there is something special and amazing about this spring. While mankind has the ability to withhold love, God is love—all of His activities are inexorably linked to His loving and unchanging character.

As earthly things are reflections of heavenly realities, human love, in some ways, is an image of the divine. It gives us hope that somewhere out there, a transcendent love exists that can live up to our greatest expectations. We have often been deceived by a love that looked pure, which in the end, was shown to be nothing of the sort. Though the earthly may be a reflection of the heavenly, the imperfect nature of that reflection is seen in the fact that human love is ephemeral, while the divine love is absolute. Human love is transitory; the divine love is not. The earthly thing changes with time; the heavenly thing will never change.

The Love we could not find with our eyes or grasp with our hands was always within reach of our hearts, because God Himself was always near. Resounding within the deepest chambers of our existence, in all harmony and magnificent vibrato, we could hear His voice of love singing over us if we would ever take the time to listen. Our spirit was made for the presence of God, and that spirit longs to be filled with divine and transcendent love. Mysteriously, there is a reciprocation of longing; He longs for us, as we long for Him. This is why the Scripture declares, "Come, all you who are thirsty, come to the waters."[15] Because He wants us to draw near, and He knows, without a shade of doubt, that His Spirit can quench our thirst. The well of earthly love runs dry quickly, while the spring of the heavenly love flows eternally.

The Psalmist spoke prophetically of the arid wasteland that is the human heart with particularly poignant imagery: "Some wandered in desert wastelands, finding no way to a city where they could settle. They were hungry and thirsty, and their lives ebbed away."[16] We are all searching for peace and satisfaction, and we will reach for anything that can satiate the hunger within. Now this spiritual appetite, in itself, is not evil. Desire can, after all, compel us to search for God. Furthermore, the Master Jesus pronounces a blessing on those disciples of His who have a righteous desire in their hearts: "Blessed are you who hunger now, for you will be satisfied."[17] So desire is not evil in itself, but James the brother of Jesus warns us: "each one is tempted when, by his own *evil desire*, he is dragged away and enticed. Then, after desire has conceived, it gives birth to sin; and sin, when it is full-grown, gives birth to death."[18]

So Desire, when she is dragged away and seduced by Evil, becomes the mother of Sin, and the grandmother of Death. We must keep careful watch over our naïve Desire if we truly care for her well-being, else she might be enticed and led to Evil, and not to the arms of her true love, who desires to satisfy her with only good things. We ought to realize, there are numerous things we think are able to satisfy us on a merely physical level, but among those possibilities, there may be only a few things that actually can satiate our hunger and thirst without bringing with them some detrimental effects. We may face future dysfunction, as we enjoy momentary bliss. The same fact is true on a spiritual level.

Generally, more natural foods are safer for us, but, quite often, we prefer the processed to the pure. What might seem more convenient, however, comes burdened with consequences to our physical health. Those issues might certainly take time to manifest. Even so, they will undoubtedly appear.

Furthermore, it is not surprising to find that eventually our bodies might begin to crave that which is unhealthy for us. This illustrates the point quite well: sometimes our desires are bad for our health. Yet, there are things in this world, good and pure things, which are healthier for our spirits because they are natural products of the goodness of God. These are able to satisfy us more deeply, because they have the spiritual nutrients we have for so long been lacking. Unfortunately, we often reject that supernal goodness because we have a sweet tooth for the processed and commercial evils of the world.

To attain true, spiritual progress we must admit that our internal hunger has been transformed and perverted. Beautiful, naïve Desire has been romanced by a wicked man. She has been swept off and changed into something obscene. She can be purified and restored to her former goodness and holiness. But she stands before us, naked and abused, perverted and ashamed, and if we cannot identify that there is something wrong, we are deceiving ourselves.

Man, in and of himself, is not evil. He was created good. His choices have perverted his purpose, and if no transformation occurs, he will never be able to commune with his Creator. The human spirit was designed so that man could have fellowship with God and enjoy the blessed satisfaction of His presence. Sadly though, we have been separated from our holy God because of our sin, and the spirit needs the satisfaction that can only be found in Him. If we are "poor" in our spirits, as the Scriptures and our hearts suggest, it is because we are lacking our most excellent Blessing.

When desire is perverted, the change might not always be overwhelming at first, but as time goes on, and evil wrests hold of us, the change becomes more dramatic. We see the affects of this perversion in the world today, and it is far more common than we would like to admit. The drug user, unable to be satisfied with their most typical fix, seeks to satisfy their desire with more potent drugs. The one suffering from sexual addiction, unable to be satisfied with common intercourse, engages in increasingly perverse sexual activity to curb the hunger within. And many in monogamous relationships, who at one point believed the emotional love they enjoyed with their partner was sufficient to satisfy, later became discontent and began the search for love all over again.

Eternal words speak to this sad spiritual state:

> They are darkened in their understanding and separated from the life of God...Having lost all sensitivity, they have given themselves over to sensuality so as to indulge in every kind of impurity, with a continual lust for more.[19]

These wandering souls are looking for satisfaction because of their insatiable appetites, but they are hopelessly hungry and horribly lost. They do not follow a proper compass, and their journey, with every wasted moment, becomes more and more difficult. With each depraved attempt at satisfaction, they move further away from the life of God.

However, when the human heart has an encounter with the Source of the divine love, there grows within the place that was once a dark heart a yearning for something wonderful, special, and intimate. More unique than anything it has ever known. Yet our success is hinged upon whether or not we embrace this great pursuit and commit to it with all that is in us. We long for the Divine only because He has made us hungry for His presence, and if we pursue Him with all that is in us, we will certainly be allowed to draw from this Great Fountain of Love.[20] But first, the voice of the Creator speaks to us from beyond the darkness that our eyes cannot see. "Here I am!" He says, "I stand at the door and knock. If anyone hears my voice and opens the door, I will come in and eat with him, and he with me"[21]—then, we will be satisfied.

Having questions about whether the love of God is enough to satisfy our hearts is understandable. A person who has no experience with God might be inclined to wonder whether Christians are merely exaggerating the descriptions of their religious experience. What mankind has made the divine love out to be is not fitting of what that love truly is.

With words, we paint a picture of the sublimity of God's supernal love for mankind. Upon completion, however, we find that our creation lacks the color and vibrance and brilliance of the image that only our hearts can behold. Our recollections of dreams serve as wonderful illustrations of this point. When things happen in our dreams, they often occur so inexplicably, we cannot even articulate our experiences to those closest to us. What remains in our hearts and minds is a faded image of what actually happened. Of what, in our late-night psyches, we actually felt and thought. We cannot duplicate the form or recreate the joy or terrors of the experiences. We can only remember and explain the portions of the dreams that are the most easily recalled. Any description we provide will lack the full scope of our initial experience. Yet, because we remember how unique it was, we are compelled to offer up those descriptions, no matter how feeble they might actually be.

The same is true in regard to the greatness of God's love. We have tasted certain things to be true of it on a spiritual level, and we use our words and concepts to translate those ideas and experiences into the realm of the physical and the mental. The greatness of the experience, though, transcends all thought, speculation, and explanation. We try our best to paint the picture, but the best we can hope for is that our words might direct others toward its beauty. Since neither God nor His love can be explained sufficiently, we must each wait for our own moment of revelation and bliss, when the great divide between the reality of His love and our own simple desire is crossed by the open and humble heart.

The span of that divide exists because of the transcendence of God; He is truly indescribable, and neither word nor thought can properly capture the beauty of the divine Glory for which our spirits are longing. That is not to say that everyone desires God, but everyone desires something, and the ultimate source of that desire is God. Yet our words and our vain imaginations have emasculated the potency of His love and made it out to be something common. Because of our feeble imaginations and our obscene desires, our hearts do not have the wherewithal, or the courage, to tell us with passion and truth and holy desire: "God's love is what I want."

The issue today is probably that when we talk about God and religion (Christianity in particular) most people have in mind only the moral standards while excluding the mystical promises of spiritual satisfaction and eternal life. The Christian's glorious message is a distinct one: The greatest experience of the human existence is available to the entire world. Before us *all* is the opportunity to bask in God's loving presence in this world and more fully in "the world to come." Experience is to our faith what blood is to the body. It fills our spiritual life with nourishment and vitality; without it, we could not survive. God is the animating force that makes our religion vibrant, meaningful, and true. Without Him, we would never truly be "alive."

God is mysterious, but He is certainly also a God of self-expression. Because of this wonderful fact, from behind the clouds of mystery, He shines forth a revelation of His love. Because He cares, He takes the time to tell us something. With words from one of His anointed, He paints us a picture of His love: "For great is your love, higher than the heavens; your faithfulness reaches to the skies."[22] He uses an illustration from nature to describe His love, and so makes us wonder whether the creation itself—the entirety of this universe that we cannot measure—is a picture of the grandeur of His love. A divine love that is limitless: A three-dimensional form that expresses what language cannot—the greatness of God and the magnitude of His divine affection.

For if God's presence is everywhere, we can know that He enfolds all of creation, there is no limit to His Presence, and certainly no limit to His love. Perhaps the universe is not only a picture of His glory, power and grand design, but perhaps it too is an image of love. More massive and stifling than anything we could imagine. Endless, enfolding, and always around us. In that respect, the universe is not an expression of divine opulence or the sad product of an insecure and ostentatious Creator. On the contrary, the universe affirms to us the truths revealed in Scripture: "God's invisible qualities—his eternal power and divine nature—"[23] It is a picture of transcendence that eons ago God Himself painted with His own hand for all of His creation to enjoy. Truly, "at night He undraws the curtain,"[24] and we can again look out into the universe and see just how vast those "heavens" are that His love surpasses. Somewhere within that vastness we exist, much like the earth. Created and fixed, established and very special to God.

This divine excellence also reminds me of the Old Testament story of Joseph in Egypt. He was in charge of counting the grain that was to go in the storehouses to help support the people of Egypt during a time of famine that the Lord had revealed was coming upon the land.[25] There was so much grain that Joseph was overwhelmed by the effort; it was too abundant for him to measure. Likewise, God's love is greater than all our limited notions, bigger than all our small hopes, and more wonderful than all our vain desires.

We were created to worship God and were formed in His image. We exist for His good pleasure and were knit together with the presence of the Divine in mind. We were made to be inhabited and God longs to fill our hearts with His love.

Certainly, what is finite was made for the Infinite. What is measureable was made for the Immeasurable. What is visible was made for the Invisible. We were formed by God for a magnificent purpose; His transcendent nature is sufficiently able to satisfy all of our spiritual desire. His beauty, glory and love surpass all that exists, and mankind was made to enjoy His presence. When we discover this Source of infinite love, we will have found all that we need to be unbelievably happy forever.

Here we are introduced to what one of our teachers calls the soul's paradox of love.[26] To find God and still to pursue Him, to be satisfied by Him but still to crave the continuous satisfaction of His presence, to know Him, yet still to long to know Him better—this is the paradox of love. While I say that He is able to satisfy our deepest desire, that He is the One who longs to be the aim of every soul's effort, I do not mean that when we find Him our desire will end. I mean that He is forever the aim toward which all our spiritual longings should be directed, and should forever be the Object of all our spiritual desires.

No matter how deep into His presence we press, we will always be able to press deeper. We will always be reaching out to touch the heart of a God who is, in majesty, awe and transcendence, infinitely far away. He is beyond us, but He is also with us. God's transcendence is not a truth we should despise, but rather, it is a celestial blessing in which we should rejoice. This was the perspective shared by Nicholas of Cusa, the late Christian mystic, who wrote of this fact centuries ago:

> I perceive that the reason wherefore Thou, O God, art unknown to all creatures, is that they may have in this divine ignorance a greater rest, as in a treasure beyond reckoning, and inexhaustible. For he who findeth a treasure that he knoweth to be utterly beyond reckoning and unlimited is moved by far greater joy than he who findeth one that may be counted, and that is limited...Thus Thou, O God, art very infinity, for which alone I yearn in every desire.[27]

Therefore, as we consider the magnitude of His love, we are forced to withdraw our misinformed thoughts and hope again for a visitation of revelation that will satisfy our deepest desire. If we could taste the glories of Heaven we would know, without a doubt, we were made for God. We would realize, and be compelled to tell others because of our newfound joy, that His love is what our spirits need. We must cry out for the presence of God and seek Him with all our heart, because, after all, His love is the end of desire.

"One thing I ask of the LORD, this is what I seek: that I may dwell in the house of the LORD all the days of my life, to gaze upon the beauty of the LORD and to seek him in his temple…My heart says of you, 'Seek his face!' Your face, LORD, I will seek."
Psalm 27:4, 8

THEY SHALL SEE GOD

THOUGHTS ON THE DEPRAVITY OF THE HUMAN HEART
AND THE NEED FOR TRANSFORMATION

"'This is what the LORD says: 'Cursed is the one who trusts in man, who depends on flesh for his strength and whose heart turns away from the LORD. He will be like a bush in the wastelands; he will not see prosperity when it comes. He will dwell in the parched places of the desert, in a salt land where no one lives….' The heart is deceitful above all things and beyond cure. Who can understand it?" Jeremiah 17:5-6, 9

Very rarely do I see myself as I really am. I have learned to look past my shortcomings and imperfections to focus on the good things, the admirable qualities. However, no one buys a diamond because it has beauty and still finds value in the flaws. We do not purchase precious stones and then ignore the blemishes. If we found gold that was tarnished, we would place it in the fire to cleanse it, to refine it, to make it pure. I am blessed and liberated, because today I see myself as I am, and I know that I need to be transformed.

I have looked into the mirror of God's Word and seen behind my fleshly eyes the eyes of evil. His image is there, and as faint as it seems, I can look back and realize the image has always been there—"he," that sinful man with all his evil desires and ungodly passions, has left some undesirable marks and I am finally ready and willing to be cleansed. The sad truth is that we are filled with all different kinds of evil, God is not pleased because of it, and it must be dealt with in true, spiritual confrontation if we are to experience the fullness of love divine.

We have before us the promise of a new life and a new love, but we must put the old heart to rest, with all its evil, hatred, and perversion. We must, like the prophet Elijah on Mount Carmel, call down fire from Heaven to manifest the glory of the true God on the evil man in our hearts. We must, like the Levites who stood on the Lord's side in the days of Moses, confront our inner selves with a sword of holiness and with a fiery zeal, slaying everything within that corrupts and perverts and delays our enjoyment of God's glorious presence in our hearts.

Even today I see my enemy. He raises his head and thinks I will not deal with him as his deeds deserve. He has become accustomed to me dealing liberally with him and giving him room to work, enjoying in part at least the fruits of his labor. But I have grown tired of his antics, and I am ready for him to die what I know will be a slow and painful death for both him and I. I will place the man on a cross and deny him his guilty pleasures and wicked desires; when his strength subsides, I will find increasing freedom and satisfaction because I put to death him who might be my greatest enemy. I tolerated him and cooperated with him on more occasions than I can recall, and ignored the fact that our relationship needed to change. But now the Lord has shown me that deceiver must be dealt with.

Perhaps the most difficult thing for most people to admit is that there is a part of them that needs to be changed; that there is a tendency inside of them that, if left unchecked, would have a tremendously negative impact on their lives. No need for demons to possess and torment us, we do the job well enough on our own. It is only by the grace and the goodness of God that our wicked tendencies do not totally ransack our lives, but they definitely have their fun, and always at our expense.

"The heart is deceitful above all things and beyond cure. Who can understand it?" The Scriptures tell us consistently that there is something wrong with the human heart that leads it into all kinds of evil, and because of that troubling fact, it must be broken, cleansed, and changed. Both Old and New Testaments of the Holy Scriptures carry within their text the same, uniform message. Of those who do not know God, the apostle Paul says: "to those who are corrupted and do not believe, nothing is pure. In fact, both their minds and consciences are corrupted. They claim to know God, but by their actions they deny him."[28] The weeping prophet Jeremiah, inspired by the precious Holy Spirit, wrote the very words of God: "wash the evil from your heart and be saved. How long will you harbor wicked thoughts?"[29] And just before our Maker covered the earth in water to purify it in the days of Noah, He was profoundly troubled by man's iniquity:

> The LORD saw how great man's wickedness on the earth had become, and that every inclination of the thoughts of his heart was only evil all the time. The LORD was grieved that he had made man on the earth, and his heart was filled with pain.[30]

The message is consistent, repeated, and defended with evidence. Thankfully, while the Scriptures declare, without regard for our feelings, that there is something obscenely wrong with us, they also speak of a promise of inward transformation that leads to a glorious and divine experience with the heart of God.

There is a purification of our hearts that must take place in order for us to experience the glories of the divine love. A holy God does not want to meet us in a sanctuary of evil. No, this God, although He loves us as we are, cannot meet us and fellowship with us in an ungodly place. For this reason, our hearts need to be changed.

Most of us have uttered some misinformed things about God's divine nature and the character of His love—things very far from the truth. We certainly did not think we were speaking foolishly, because in our hearts we sincerely believed the things we said. Therein, we discover the heart of the issue, or rather, the issue of the heart. Our earliest and simplest religion is a function of our hearts, and we create our virtue and our gods based upon the things we have stored up in our hearts. Our most primitive images of the divine love are taken from the virtue we ourselves create, and not from true, spiritual insight. When those illusions are confronted with genuine spiritual truth, then the battle for our souls begins.

Our thinking, our feeling, and our desire *must* be confronted and transformed. This is why the Scripture says, "The LORD detests the thoughts of the wicked, but those of the pure are pleasing to him."[31]

Yet, so often we acquiesce to our emotions, desires, and inclinations. We say that our desire is who we are. But we should not confuse human desire with basic animal instinct. We are too often defined by our desires. We succumb to the primal longings of that old man of sin within. Yet, as humans, we can choose. We may one day be tempted to steal, but we can choose not to. We would not, for one moment, say because our desire to steal was so strong "This is who I am"—and those standing in judgment would not absolve our behavior based on a supposed slavery to depravity.

Others might find themselves having to fight the urge to molest young girls or young boys, but we would not find ourselves agreeing to the foolishness of thinking they are doomed, or even worse, created by God to be a child molester. We live in a fallen world indeed, and we have deceitful hearts, which tempt us and drive us toward damnable and unconscionable things.

The testimony of God Himself is that there are some thoughts that are pleasing to Him, and others that He does not enjoy. Our hearts are sick, and they need to be healed. Jesus Christ explained the problem to His disciples:

> What comes out of a man is what makes him 'unclean,' said Jesus. For from within, out of men's hearts, come evil thoughts, sexual immorality, theft, murder, adultery, greed, malice, deceit, lewdness, envy, slander, arrogance and folly. All these evils come from inside and make a man 'unclean.'[32]

Indeed, it is our hearts that deceive us and lead us to believe that we can approach God and serve Him in any way we choose, and thereby gain the richness of an experience with His divine love in return. The idea that we can be free of guilt when we live in a way that so openly contradicts God's glorious ideal is absurd and sad. It also assumes there is a god who exists that cares very little for the way His creatures conduct themselves. Yet I assure you, this is not the case. The frailty of the human spirit does not demean the value that the Divine places on the human heart. While He may be displeased with it, He can still desire it. He does, however, stand much like a lover betrayed by his sweetheart. After learning of an indiscretion, the man can still desire the woman with all his heart, but still, deep down he is repulsed by her unfaithfulness. We are still divinely desired; nonetheless, a holy God is divinely displeased.

We have a standard toward which we have been encouraged to strive: a new heart that God desires to give us, new passions that God wants to birth within us, and a pure love that God desires us to know and enjoy forever. It is up to us, however, to recognize the poverty of our spirits and pray to God for a visitation of revelation that can transform the old into the new; a vision of heavenly light that will remove us from the darkness of sin into the light of life. Otherwise, in the end of days, we might find ourselves falling under the same judgment as those mentioned in the Word from Heaven. And because of our spiritual neglect, we will be excluded from enjoying the glories of God. We should hope that we are not so foolish:

> The wrath of God is being revealed from heaven against all the godlessness and wickedness of men who suppress the truth by their wickedness...although they knew God, they neither glorified him as God nor gave thanks to him, but their thinking became futile and their foolish hearts were darkened. Although they claimed to be wise, they became fools.[33]

We know the righteous ideal that God has set before us; we have knowledge of what He loves and that which He hates. But our duplicitous hearts have betrayed us. Our other selves have lied to us, making us believe that God is not righteous and holy, and letting us feel comfortable with lives we knew needed to be changed long ago. Our hearts have encouraged us to exchange the glory of the immortal God, and therefore defined the divine love in simple and unholy terms. They have painted a picture of a god who does not exist, and they have titled the icon that they have created, "The Lord of Heaven and Earth."

If they could see into the Heavens, they would cower in fear at the Lord's response to their abominable creation. In Heaven above, the Lord sits on His throne and is filled with anger because of their presumption, and He warns us through

His eternal Word with a message of disgust saying "You thought that I was one like you."[34] But His eyes are too pure to look upon evil,[35] and He is not pleased. We have created, in our ignorance, a god who cannot satisfy; He is not infinite, but impotent. He is not a God of righteousness, peace, and love, but a god of indulgence, revelry, and injustice. It is no wonder our religions do not satisfy. We heard the Word sent down from Heaven, but our hearts resisted any change. I have judged my heart and its unholy desires, and my God has rendered His righteous verdict: "It is time for that deceiver to die!"

Our old hearts have failed us, and our lives are now spent. We must place ourselves on a cross to die, and pray for God to revive us with a new source of life from Heaven. All of us must receive a new heart, able to grow and change as God wills: a pure heart, in which an undefiled love can be poured by the Holy Spirit, and from which it can be shared with the world.

Even so, the impression of the old heart and our old ways will remain in our memories and in our bodies even when we are given new hearts. We will remember their empty promises, and the times they disappointed us by failing to satisfy our souls. Our old passions may still tempt us, but receiving a new heart is a wonderful beginning, it is a safe time to start searching for spiritual satisfaction in a chaotic and confusing world. We must have the courage to sing the song of David and acknowledge before God in Heaven that, in honor of His holiness, we long to be different. Let us ponder the words of Jesus and ask the Lord to give us clean hearts, because He said "Blessed are the pure in heart, for they shall see God."[36]

"Have mercy on me, O God, according to your unfailing love; according to your great compassion blot out my transgressions. Wash away all my iniquity and cleanse me from my sin. For I know my transgressions, and my sin is always before me…Create in me a pure heart, O God, and renew a steadfast spirit within me."
Psalm 51:1-3, 10

DEEP AND HIDDEN THINGS

THOUGHTS ON EXPERIENCING THE DIVINE MYSTERY AND LEARNING THE SECRET THINGS OF GOD

"Can you fathom the mysteries of God? Can you probe the limits of the Almighty? They are higher than the heavens—what can you do? They are deeper than the depths of the grave—what can you know? Their measure is longer than the earth and wider than the sea." Job 11:7-9

At its core, Christianity is a mystical tradition; a religion established and passed on with the idea in mind that the mysterious can and should be experienced personally. Its teachings are predicated on the assumption that there is an entire world that exists invisibly, and that world affects us in ways we cannot fully understand. Yet that invisible world can and should be touched and embraced by our hearts. This is something that most spiritual seekers ignore about the Christian faith. It has been categorized for so many years as a simple tradition by the media, and by those who supposedly embraced it as their own at some time, only to find disappointment and not true, spiritual fulfillment.

Nevertheless, the richness of the Christian heritage is living still. It is a living faith connected to a living God and King—eternal, immortal, invisible. Because of this divine presence, the deepest and truest experience of one who has wholeheartedly embraced this faith as their own is powerful, intense, and has, as its fruit, an ever-increasing satisfaction.

Even Christianity's spiritual predecessor, Judaism, held the same truth about the invisible world in high regard as attested to by the words of the Law:

> Hear, O Israel: The LORD our God, the LORD is one. Love the LORD your God with all your heart and with all your soul and with all your strength. These commandments that I give you today are to be upon your hearts. Impress them on your children. Talk about them when you sit at home and when you walk along the road, when you lie down and when you get up. Tie them as symbols on your hands and bind them on your foreheads. Write them on the doorframes of your houses and on your gates.[37]

Not only were the Jews of old taught to affirm the truth of their God and to walk faithfully in His ways, but they were also taught to love Him and to keep the fact of His presence in mind, no matter where they were. Invisible though He may be, He can and should be experienced personally in our lives.

This teaching implied the idea that the invisible was just as real as the visible, for they served a God whom, in essence, they could not see, but who asked for their sincere devotion nonetheless. That invisible God expected them to love Him with all of their being, and He promised that if they did, He would remain as their King and their Rock forever. So with heart and soul and mind, their devotion was to be fixed on their invisible and wonderful Maker.

Those who passed on the aforementioned teachings about Israel's relation to the Divine One understood they were receiving insight and revelation from a Being who is greater than anything they could imagine, because they knew that He alone was the Originator of all that is.

Those descendants who followed the promised Messiah, Jesus Christ, had the same mindset, and one of them was inspired to pen the following words: "by him all things were created: things in heaven and on earth, visible and invisible, whether thrones or powers or rulers or authorities; all things were created by him and for him. He is before all things, and in him all things hold together."[38]

Christians are well acquainted with the Divine Mystery. They believe that He can be known more fully by those who seek Him, but also that He wants to be known by them as well. That is why the Scripture says that "without faith it is impossible to please God, because anyone who comes to him must believe that he exists and that he rewards those who earnestly seek him."[39] Thus, their tradition holds to the message that the mysterious can be experienced and that this supernatural knowledge, if we respond appropriately, has the power to change our lives.

It is the defined nature of mystery to arouse intrigue and curiosity; it moves us to speculate about things we cannot readily know. In regard to understanding our mysterious Maker and the nuances of the mystical religion that He has given to mankind to direct them to Himself, there is a strange paradox that exists. God's glory is truly incomprehensible, and His transcendent qualities are impossible for our minds to grasp on their own. This is why in one place someone inquires:

> Can you fathom the mysteries of God? Can you probe the limits of the Almighty? They are higher than the heavens—what can you do? They are deeper than the depths of the grave—what can you know?[40]

While in another place we are told that "if you call out for insight and cry aloud for understanding, and if you look for it as for silver and search for it as for hidden treasure, then you will understand the fear of the LORD and find the knowledge of God."[41] Fortunately, the mystery does not deter us completely. The curious part of our nature still wants to delve deeper into the mystery; it longs to discover that "hidden treasure" and sees the gloriousness of searching out that abstruse mystery even today. Both of the Scriptures convey equal truth, but there is a spiritual medium by which we can reconcile the paradox.

We do not know God as we should. We know Him casually, as we know the postman or the grocer, and when we address Him we are cordial and brief. There is no particular urgency inspiring a relationship. We may speak with Him on occasion, but only out of habit or some sense of obligation. His friendship is not one we truly value, and as such, we do not feel like expending the energy it will require to get to know Him a bit better.

We know God vaguely from the very muddled and mixed information we hear, think and read. Then, we develop our own spirituality, theology, and worldview upon those disjointed pieces, most of which are not meant to fit together.

We have sought to join those pieces together as in a puzzle, yet when we realize some important pieces are missing, we just find the nearest puzzle we can and take pieces that fit only when forced and twisted. The final product is not a proper reflection of spiritual truth, but we do not mind because the fill-ins we found made our job a little easier, and it actually created a picture we preferred. It became an image we appreciated much more than the real thing.

In the end, we rest comfortably with whatever image we have created because it requires far less effort on our part. Then, we enjoy a god we have created on our own and wonder why our lives are so unfulfilled.

Sadly, we do not know our Heavenly Father, and that is our greatest error. He is mysterious, and for this reason, the Scripture uses figurative language to describe His appearance by saying, "Clouds and thick darkness surround him...."[42] His veiled nature is not something we should despise, however, because this divine mystery makes God far more compelling than the simple gods we create for ourselves.

Obscurity only enhances God's glory, and makes the distinction between humanity and Divinity far more pronounced. It shows us that God is different from common and earthly things, that He is uniquely worthy of our devotion. Nevertheless, He can, and should still, be known to us as we seek genuine spiritual truth and nothing else. The fact that His nature is obscure and transcendent does not mean that we cannot understand Him at all. If that were the case we would not be in error if we created our own counterfeit god to supplant a God that cannot be known personally any way.

If in our country, no concrete currency existed, I imagine there would be no such thing as counterfeiting. As it is, because an established currency does exist, trying to replicate that currency to suit your own interests is considered a punishable offense. Likewise, an established God exists, and counterfeiting Him is a sign of disrespect and a blatant neglect for the laws of the universe.

The Divine Mystery does not permit us to create our own likenesses of His glory for personal use, but rather, He is set apart and honored in distinction because of His lofty nature. As such, He should not be treated as a common commodity.

Be that as it may, God is a God of self-expression, and the prophet Daniel spoke from a higher perspective when he reconciled the earlier paradox for us all by his inspired words: "there is a God in heaven who reveals mysteries."[43] We should look to this Great Source of eternal wisdom, who rules His people from Heaven, because "He gives wisdom to the wise and knowledge to the discerning...He knows what lies in the darkness, and light dwells with Him."[44]

Then the Voice from Heaven speaks again to confirm the words of the prophet: "the Lord gives wisdom, and from his mouth come knowledge and understanding."[45] Through His Spirit and His Word, He enables us to peer into the Divine mystery. He reveals to us "the secret things of God,"[46] and enables our eyes to behold the clarity of His truth. Each glimpse makes us more curious, and each vision of truth works to sanctify our hearts, transforming us from the inside out. The pieces of that grand puzzle were mysteriously missing, but they were certainly near; we only needed to put forth the effort to find them and we had to decide in our hearts that no other pieces would do.

The contemplation of the mysterious is an inseparable part of our human experience, no matter the spiritual tradition to which we have pledged our lives. Curiosity is not an attribute of Jews, Hindus, Christians or Muslims alone, but mankind as a whole. We were made with a curious nature: to wonder about the universe, to contemplate the Divine. Indeed, every time we withdraw from our hurried lives to meditate on the greatness and the goodness of God, we are treading upon the realm of Mystery, approaching the unapproachable, but something within us all bids us to go forward. Our desire begs us not to stop until we have the knowledge for which we search, the love that our hearts need, the hidden treasure that must be found.

Wonderful, new experiences await those who diligently seek God.[47] There is an exceedingly great reward to be had if we are willing to spend the time, the faithfulness, and the passion that it will cost for us to behold the mystery of love.

But as with any great venture, if there is a great reward available, there is also great risk. There is a danger that lies on the trek toward the mysterious. We may, unfortunately, like a ship without an anchor caught in the midst of a great storm, find our hearts and minds in unfamiliar and dangerous territory, headed toward assumptions, conclusions, and so-called revelations that will lead our hearts, and the hearts of others, astray. We may find ourselves tossed about by every wind of teaching and new philosophy that claims to know "The Truth," and even some that claim, foolishly, that "truth cannot be known."

It is no wonder that the apostle Paul told his friend and pupil Timothy to "Watch your life and your doctrine closely."[48] Else, Timothy too may have been carried off into the same treacherous waters I mentioned above, and those who followed him would have suffered the same fate. We would do well to heed the warning given so long ago. The command is timeless, and the danger is as well. Certainly, the reward for embarking on a journey as great as this is worth the risk.

Great things are in store for those who seek divine revelation, but wisdom, discernment, Scripture, and Spirit must be invited to accompany us and to guide us on our voyage. If we set out with those righteous friends absent, we will certainly find ourselves lost at sea, unable to find the way to our True Home.

If we desire a greater life, we must be willing enough to set sail our hearts toward the unknown and humble enough to follow the guiding Words of Him for whom we search. To be sure, His eternal Word is our most trustworthy map, and it will keep us safe as we set sail on our journey. As the psalmist said, God's Word is "a lamp to my feet and a light for my path."[49]

If we rely on our own bearings we will certainly find ourselves lost without remedy. Yet, like our earlier task, so many shun the effort and pick up pieces from a different puzzle to make things fit. There is, of course, no true experience with God and they are left empty and baffled by their failure. Their excitement deceived them and they settled for simple emotion, were satisfied with the presumptuous power of positive thinking, and fell for intriguing yet hollow and harmful philosophy, while never getting to taste the glory of the One who truly satisfies. Attractive though they may appear, the excitement is certainly short-lived, and the result of their erroneous practice is inevitably disappointing.

We need a fresh, new start, a mind energized by the heavenly and guided toward true, spiritual treasure; if we are hungry for Truth, perhaps He will grace us with understanding through His Word and by His Spirit.[50] So, in our thinking and in our hearts, we meditate on the mystery of love and hope so humbly that we might experience a visitation from above. We are encouraged when we remember those words of hope spoken by Daniel. "There is God in heaven who reveals mysteries," and only He reveals "deep and hidden things."[51]

> "Ask and it will be given to you; seek and you will find; knock and the door will be opened to you. For everyone who asks receives; he who seeks finds; and to him who knocks, the door will be opened." Matthew 7:7-8

-4-

A HORRIBLE MISUNDERSTANDING

THOUGHTS ON THE CHARACTER OF THE DIVINE LOVE AND UNDERSTANDING THE HOLINESS OF GOD

"Place me like a seal over your heart, like a seal on your arm; for love is as strong as death, its jealousy unyielding as the grave. It burns like blazing fire, like a mighty flame. Many waters cannot quench love; rivers cannot wash it away. If one were to give all the wealth of his house for love it would be utterly scorned."
Song of Songs 8:6-7

As in a broken mirror, we see Love's face, but are forced to reverently piece together an image that we cannot fully see. So often, what we create as an image of love is not a proper likeness of the undefiled blessing found in the heart of God, enjoyed in the hearts of the faithful by the power of His Holy Spirit. I look forward, then, to a time and a place when and where we might know the divine love in a grander and a more unique way. This is when God will be closer to us than He has ever been, and where all our hopes and dreams will be satisfied as we rest joyfully in His bosom forever. When the conflagration of the heavenly love will consume its earthly counterpart, and where righteousness will rule for ever after the final advent of Jesus Christ. But it is this same Jesus who tells His disciples that the world will know them by their love.[52] In the centuries since our Savior's death, though, how appealing does the "love" we have shown look to the world?

There is something to be said about professed Christians failing to represent the message of Jesus of Nazareth, but media outlets today do not make the issue any less complicated. They confound the problem by highlighting only our frailty, all the while, the good works associated with Christ's love are overlooked and ignored. We are mocked and scorned, yet even our Master told us that the world would hate us because of Him. So the methods they employ should not surprise us in the least.

Nevertheless, some of the ridicule we experience we have brought upon ourselves. We must return to holiness, we must once again be concerned with the needs of others more so than those of ourselves, we must rekindle the flame of love and remind ourselves that we are "the light of the world."[53] So, we must take our licks and turn our cheeks and accept the ridicule when we do and do not deserve it. And as much as we have opportunity, we should show kindness and mercy and care to all men, that they may see our good deeds and our genuine love, and glorify the Father of all.[54]

Still, there are enough genuine Christians in the world, who love and give and are merciful to even their enemies that I am proud to call them my brothers and sisters in Christ, and I can say that our message is true, because I know it has power to transform hearts and lives. Some of the legitimate people of God have, by their actions, left visible marks on the world. Mother Theresa, Martin Luther King, Jr., and William Wilberforce are only three examples of a faithful nation, whose King is Jesus, who moved the foundations of the world and showed us the character of love divine.

The character of love lies in the impression that it leaves on those with whom it has come in contact. It is the expression of the true nature of the Divine. We can observe the mark that real love leaves on the world—its truest and most honest expression, reflected in the results it produces. Mother Theresa reached out to the unloved and uncared for masses in Calcutta, Martin Luther King, Jr. played a pivotal role in helping to advance the cause of civil rights in the U.S., and William Wilberforce was so strongly convicted by his Christian virtue that He fought to abolish slavery in England for decades.

While these examples are memorable and historical, they were all inspired by the actions of their Master, Jesus Christ. The premier expression of divine love was seen in the offering of Jesus: it was love that motivated His sacrifice, and love that saw it through to the finish. The most valuable Being in the universe offered Himself for the poorest of people. Graciously, the love that He poured out by His blood makes those who have been sprinkled by it the wealthiest spirits on earth. Finances and possessions make no difference in our kingdom, and it should make no difference in our hearts; what we have received and what we now enjoy is priceless and indescribable. He stands forever as The Lover of the Universe, and because of this love, generations have wholeheartedly put their hope in Him. This premier expression of love produced innumerable and priceless fruit. We, who have experienced it in glory, know this to be so.

There are millions today who have experienced this love personally and can attest to the veracity of its affection and the purity of its fiery passion. Furthermore, they not only felt this love and enjoyed it in their hearts, but they were compelled to share it with the world around them through kind, gentle, and brave works. Large and small, their exploits were performed in the service of Jesus Christ, for the benefit of all mankind. Even so, the world at large has a very simple notion about the love Christians claim to covet.

We cannot know God's love completely—that is, there will always remain a glimmer of mystery, no matter how much insight we gain. The finite mind cannot grasp the glories of an infinite love. In order for love to be divine it must be, in a way, mysterious and transcendent. If God could be known completely, He would not be as special as we claim. Likewise, if His love were as simple as we may sometimes make it seem, it would not be the end of our spiritual desire.

All the symbols and the shadows we see in Scripture, and all the images we create, can never match the true glory of the transcendent God and His tender heart of love. But they are indeed helpful; they help the mind apprehend what only the spirit and the heart can truly enjoy. That being said, it is a definite possibility for a person to come to a mature understanding of God's heart of love if they are willing to spend the time in study and fellowship with God it will take for that knowledge to be gained. We cannot know everything, but we can certainly know a lot. He can give us wisdom through His eternal Word, and He can enlighten our hearts by His Spirit.

All the same, His love, transcending emotion and feeling, is so remarkable that I used to find myself aggravated by the fact that the only word we have for it today is "love." We use the term so often to refer to so many different things. For example, of a favorite movie we might say, "I *love* that movie," or even referring to a car we might say, "I *love* that car." To a close friend or a special someone, we might say, "I *love* you." Yet when we use this word loosely to express different ideas, do we dishonor the quality of the Divine in our thinking? Do we confuse the mind as we tickle the heart and fail to set apart God's love as holy?

Perhaps the frequent use of this word is not as harmful as it may seem. By that I mean, perhaps the fact that the word blankets our culture is a positive rather than a negative: across the world "love" is getting our attention. Furthermore, the word itself is not as important anyway as understanding the Mystery to which the word is connected. This is the greater issue. Words are connected to concepts and ideals. The word itself is benign—the meaning holds the beauty.

"Words are only the outward image of truth and can never be the inward essence. Words are incidental."[55] So when we speak of God's *love*, the divine *love*, or God *loving* us, we should always have in mind the truth that when used in reference to the Holy One, the meaning carries with it all the hopes, desires, and the hungers of mankind. We need love: not the word, but the truth—the divine beauty that the word denotes.

If the issue is not particularly with the mechanics of our words, then what causes us most of our problems in regard to properly understanding the mystery of love? Well, television shows, books, movies and various other sources have all given us vague and disjointed images of "God," "love," and "religion." In many ways, truth is boring, and some falsehoods seem to suit our very human need for entertainment far better than the truth. Each day we are bombarded with erroneous notions of who our Maker is. As a result of this constant confusion, the truth that should rest behind our words is often lost.

It has taken me some time to learn a simple truth: God is holy. As I learned what that holiness implied, I began to use the word *holy* in connection to the divine love. In doing so, I began to pour into my knowledge of that love all that I knew of God's holiness, and did my best to destroy my delusions, while using His Word as a filter to sift truth from error.

We can call His love holy in the most divine sense of the word because it is part of God's unitary nature: an attribute—something we know to be true of God. Not something He has, even though we often imply that with our words, but something He *is*. "God is love" is the truth that our Scripture declares in 1 John, though it can be said that this teaching is expressed throughout the entirety of the written Word. Truly, the divine love is the expression of God's nature toward us, and from Genesis to Revelation this truth is evident.[56] Therefore, this divine love shares the same immutable qualities as God, because God loving us is simply God being Himself.

Now, to understand what we mean when we say that God's love is holy, let us consider what holiness implies. When speaking of our great high priest Jesus, the writer of Hebrews makes this statement about the Messiah and gives us a picture of the holiness of God: "Such a high priest meets our need—one who is *holy, blameless, pure, set apart from sinners, exalted above the heavens.*"[57] Before He makes this statement, though, He tells us "The Son is the radiance of God's glory and the exact representation of his being."[58] So we perceive the expression of divine holiness by observing Jesus of Nazareth.

Therefore, if love is holy just as God is holy, it must be blameless, pure, set apart from sinners, and exalted (in God) above the heavens. For this reason, we must perceive God's love only "in the splendor of His holiness." Now, that holiness means two things that we ought to understand: 1) In position and majesty, God is far above the heavens and the earth, He is exalted as King far above His creation, and 2) In quality of nature and personality, God is completely pure and separate from sin and evil. In Him is infinite goodness and perfection, of which we cannot even comprehend. God is holy; He is infinitely unique, flawless, and will never need to change.

We see love connected to this holiness in Scripture:

"Jehoshaphat appointed men to sing to the LORD and to praise him for *the splendor of his holiness* as they went out at the head of the army, saying: 'Give thanks to the LORD, *for his love endures forever.*'"[59] They praised the Lord in the splendor of His holiness, while calling attention to His everlasting love. Everything that God is, we know to be holy and set apart. So when we think of the divine love, we must set it apart in our minds and our hearts as holy, pure, set apart from sinners and exalted above the heavens. If we do not sanctify this love in our thoughts and lives, our ideas of love, which come from an unholy world, will be simple and incomplete, and will lead us to some unfortunate mistakes in life.

Certainly, the Creator is the source of all pure, human forms of love as well, as He is the One who gave mankind its emotional composition. His divine love, however, is totally distinct from any love that proceeds from the humanity of man. It is gloriously unique. Just as He created a human spirit that cannot approach the glory of His Holy Spirit, so too did He grant humans the capacity for natural human love that cannot approach the glory of His divine love. It might share some similar characteristic qualities, but this is only to point our hearts toward Heaven, in search of the love that satisfies forever. Our love is imperfect; His love is thoroughly divine.

Scripture teaches us a truth about God's disposition most would like to discount. We pass on the message of a soft and gentle God—which He very much is—but are afraid to accept those terrible things mentioned in Scripture about His character. The popular conception that our idea of God was created to breed fear, and thus, in a time such as this, we need to be liberated from it, is simple-minded to say the least. If our God is truly God, His nature is fearsome and awesome and terrible in the truest sense of the words. If He is not those things, He could not possibly be God.

If we were trapped in the wilderness in the middle of a fire and did not tremble in fear, that would not say as much about us as it would about the fire. If it is truly powerful, its power will breed terror, not because of our descriptions, simply because of its nature. A god who is not frightening is impotent, and that type of god is not worthy of my service or devotion. God has no true power if we can stand before the fire of His presence and not feel the least bit of anxiety in front of the Great Power that forged heaven and earth. So, we must hold fast to the truth of who God has revealed Himself to be. To do otherwise would be to disrespect His character. And this He does not enjoy.

Sadly, our failure to recognize God's holiness and to obey Him in reverent fear leads us toward evil. In the prophet Ezekiel's day, His anger burned against the Israelites, and His words to them were a warning for the whole earth to heed:

> There is a conspiracy of her princes within her like a roaring lion tearing its prey; they devour people, take treasures and precious things and make many widows within her. Her priests do violence to my law and profane my holy things; they do not distinguish between the holy and the common; they teach that there is no difference between the unclean and the clean...I am profaned among them...The people of the land practice extortion and commit robbery; they oppress the poor and needy and mistreat the alien, denying them justice.[60]

So often today we profane God's law; we do not distinguish between the common and the uncommon. In doing so, much evil has been perpetrated in the name of God that was not motivated by God at all. Christianity has been blamed for many of the evils seen in the world, but God's law and His direction lead righteous hearts toward positive results and holy activities, things that the entire world needs to see. Oppression, mistreatment, and injustice result from our refusal to honor the holiness of God and to live our lives in a way that pleases Him, reflecting the truth of that holiness.

There are groups of so-called Christians that want to escape the boundaries of tradition and blame the problems of our world on the lack of progressive thinking within the Church of God. Yet, if our foundation is truly in Christ, it is not in the future, it was established in the past. To change the true Church and to make it "more progressive," we would first need to go back to Jerusalem and tell Jesus Christ not to die for the sins of the world. We would have to tell Him that 2,000 years later His teachings and those of His disciples will grow old and out of touch with the culture. We would have to tell Jesus that we do not want Him; we want to change our foundations. We do not want His blood that sanctified us in truth, because truth is relative, and He is no longer relevant in our world.

So this is what these new progressive groups would have to say to Jesus. Indeed, this is what they are already telling Him today. I am fairly young myself, but I do not agree with them. I know that Jesus has helped and not hurt the world. I know that His true disciples, the faithful remnant, have loved the world much. And I want to be very much like them.

But these progressive Christians might pose the question as evidence to their claims, "How many wars in recent history were fought in the name of Christ or in the name of religion?" I do not know the answer to that silly question, but I know that the Christ said "Blessed are the peacemakers, for they will be called sons of God."[61] So I do not blame Jesus Christ for any wars, or any violence, because I believe that His words are still relevant and true today. And I believe that His true disciples will always remember and do their best to apply His words to their lives. If I do blame anyone for the world's problems and its lack of love, I blame unholy people with unholy passions that pervert holy ideals to sanctify their evil deeds. I believe this is why God cares so much about holiness: because holiness keeps us from evil, and a failure to recognize holiness is the reason for all the problems of our world.

The reason why "the fear of the Lord is the beginning of wisdom,"[62] is because we can only live rightly before a God we reverence and respect. That word *fear* indicates a reverent love, as well as a sober terror. The God who hates sin loves the sad people who practice it, but as we honor Him in holiness, and are wise enough to understand we ought not to live in any way we choose, our lives will begin to blossom into righteousness. God will then pluck us from the garden of a dying world, and use us to adorn His fallen creation until His Son returns.

The "Church" has been blamed for a lot over the centuries. But only because the world does not understand that the Church is not an incorporated organization, or a power that formerly controlled nations and kingdoms and peoples, nor is it a group that terrorizes the lost masses with hate and unrighteous judgment, or persecutes confused homosexuals and lost little girls who take the lives of their unborn babies. No, the Church of Jesus Christ that I know is an invisible and holy entity. It is a supernatural kingdom established by the blood of Jesus Christ, filled with people who are called to be slaves to love and truth and peace, and they are "the salt of the earth." Their holiness preserves the world, keeps it from destruction, and gives it a flavor of goodness. They are gentle and meek, and have pledged their lives to righteousness. They are not afraid to call wrong "wrong," and right "right." However, they will not be evil toward those who practice evil, by their goodness and their tender love, they will exhort people toward righteous living, and they will lead by their example. This is the Church that I know—not perfect, but holy, and set apart by God. So we better stop blaming the people of God, the servants of Jesus Christ, because those people are holy, and we know how God feels about His holy things and His holy people.

Our failure to honor God's holiness has led us to duplicity. How often has the word "love" been used to sanctify all kinds of perversion? People are hungry for love, yet in regard to our personal relationships and our religious and spiritual experiences, we fail to distinguish between the false and the true.

Accordingly, it leads to disheartening results and dreadful experiences for people all over the world. We need not throw out our hope for love; we need only realize the love for which we should be searching. We must identify the true and turn our hearts from anything else.

To set Himself apart as holy in the sight of Israel, God set a boundary around Mount Sinai that the people could not cross when He descended upon it. By observing the boundaries in obedience, the Israelites set Yahweh apart and honored His holiness. The separation between the mountain and the people represents the distinction between God's nature and our own. God, in His divinity, is far above man in his humanity. Our God of love rests at the top of Mount Sinai, while we stand far below Him in exaltation, knowing that we cannot approach the purity of who He is. We rest below Him honoring His commands and only when He calls us can we approach the place where He dwells as Moses did. Yet the distinction between the divine and the common should be a welcome landmark in our spiritual pursuit to discover our heart's desire.

The Bible is extant with examples of God's holiness. All of which help us to understand that the nature of God is pure. Accordingly, that purity is spread to those He touches by His Holy Spirit. Those who come to faith in Christ are said to be partakers "in the divine nature," and those who, by the Eternal Spirit's inward working, will "escape the corruption in the world caused by evil desires."[63] Of these same participants in godliness, it is said that God has poured His love into their hearts by His Holy Spirit. For this reason, the Scriptures provide a brief, yet insightful look into the nature of this divine attribute, as it outlines the character of the love Christians claim to know, which has been placed within their hearts, and that they are obligated to share with the world.

While the following example is not an extensive dissertation on the nature of the divine love, nor does it cover the varying forms of love mentioned in Scripture, it has, for centuries, inspired immeasurable volumes of thought on the subject:

> If I speak in the tongues of men and of angels, but have not love, I am only a resounding gong or a clanging cymbal. If I have the gift of prophecy and can fathom all mysteries and all knowledge, and if I have a faith that can move mountains, but have not love, I am nothing. If I give all I possess to the poor and surrender my body to the flames, but have not love, I gain nothing. Love is patient, love is kind. It does not envy, it does not boast, it is not proud. It is not rude, it is not self-seeking, it is not easily angered, it keeps no record of wrongs. Love does not delight in evil but rejoices with the truth. It always protects, always trusts, always hopes, always perseveres. Love never fails.[64]

In matters of time, His love is constant and eternal. What love is, it has *always* been, it is *always*, and it will *always* be. In quality, His love is pure. It is absolutely holy, unique, and special in the most amazing way possible. In integrity, it is unshakeable. What love is not, it can *never* be. It is absolutely good, and does not delight in evil. In action, it is relentless. What it does, it does *continually*. In consistency, it is unchanging. What it does not do, it *never* does. In delight, it rejoices with truth. In reaction, it is temperate and self-controlled. In power, it is unmatched. In regard to others it is hopeful, trusting, forgiving, persevering, patient, selfless, humble, calm, and honest—it always desires the best for others and is willing to act accordingly.

Certainly, the aforementioned passage is not the only image of love that God has placed before us. The Holy Scriptures carry within all their stories, poems, prophecies and letters a comprehensive and unfolding story of God's divine passion for mankind. Because we have not taken the time to study that holy Word, and we have neglected to exert ourselves by digging to find the treasure within its pages, we have a very simple notion of God and of His love.

We are so often guilty of forcing the love of God into a

box of our own distorted preconceptions and presumptions, restricted by the limits of our language and thought, so that it becomes a fleeting function of our humanity and not truly a holy gift of a divine Creator who is absolutely indescribable. We certainly have an idea of what love is or could be, but we awaken to our disillusionment when we realize that most of our ideas about God's nature, God's kingdom, and God's people rarely align themselves with spiritual truth.

Our words and our thoughts are rarely laced with a true, spiritual knowledge because we are so careless in the things that we say and so irreverent in the way in which we approach the holy things of God. With those same words we build a tower like those in Babel, hoping to reach the heights of Jehovah, doing our best to unveil the God of mystery and to explain the intricacies of His divine affection. We do this without first honoring Him in the splendor of His holiness, not knowing that our efforts will only lead to confusion. Like those spoken of in Ezekiel's book, we do not distinguish between the holy and the common and in doing so we profane the love of God. What a horrible misunderstanding.

> "I pray that out of his glorious riches he may strengthen you with power through his Spirit in your inner being, so that Christ may dwell in your hearts through faith. And I pray that you, being rooted and established in love, may have power, together with all the saints, to grasp how wide and long and high and deep is the love of Christ, and to know this love that surpasses knowledge— that you may be filled to the measure of all the fullness of God."
> Ephesians 3:16-19

HIS TREASURED POSSESSION

THOUGHTS ON THE KNOWLEDGE OF GOD AND THE REJECTION OF TRUTH

"For since the creation of the world God's invisible qualities—his eternal power and divine nature—have been clearly seen, being understood from what has been made, so that men are without excuse. For although they knew God, they neither glorified him as God nor gave thanks to him, but their thinking became futile and their foolish hearts were darkened. Although they claimed to be wise, they became fools and exchanged the glory of the immortal God…They exchanged the truth of God for a lie…."
Romans 1:20-23, 25a

Among the usual activity of humanity, progress of any kind, be it positive or negative, starts first in the soul. To begin any task, there must first be a thought, then follows the act. The essay begins with the brainstorm and then the development of a thesis statement (or main idea); the business endeavor begins with the idea, then come the proposal and the plan; the friendship begins first with the thought of affinity and then the cultivation of a relationship; and the marriage usually does not begin without there being first a thought of love. All the progress of mankind begins first with a thought, and the type of thought dictates the type of activity that follows said thought.

It is no secret, then, that a person's actions directly result from his or her thinking. The person whose thoughts are focused on sexual activity will more likely than not find themselves engaged in that same activity. Those whose thoughts are focused greatly on deceitful schemes will undoubtedly find themselves engaged in that type of activity. Likewise, those whose thoughts are righteous, holy and upright, will more likely than not find themselves engaged in that type of activity.

These outcomes are not the result of metaphysical energy that shapes our external worlds based on our thoughts, but a more simple explanation is available. You act based on what you think: your life is a function of your thinking because your thinking dictates how you live. So it should not surprise us to find out that God actually cares about what we are thinking because our thoughts control our actions and our actions shape our lives. Even our patriarch Adam considered the words of the deceiving serpent in his thoughts. It would have been impossible for him to move any appendage without first thinking to do so. With the hand he held the forbidden fruit, and with his mouth he ate of it. And we see the great consequences of his thoughts today.

Our spiritual lives are inexorably linked to the patterns of our thinking. It is not enough for us to merely ponder and contemplate spiritual concepts; we must discover and apprehend spiritual *truth*. Tozer put it wonderfully when he said:

> What comes into our minds when we think about God is the most important thing about us. The history of mankind will probably show that no people has ever risen above its religion, and man's spiritual history will positively demonstrate that no religion has ever been greater than its idea of God...the gravest question before the Church is always God Himself, and the most portentous fact about any man is not what he at a given time may say or do, but what he in his deep heart conceives God to be like...Were we able to extract from any man a complete answer to the question, 'What comes into your mind when you think about God?' we might predict with certainty the spiritual future of that man.[65]

Whether we are discussing spiritual concepts, religious ideas, or philosophical maxims, the content of our thinking is a sign of our spiritual health, or a lack thereof.

Adam's thoughts were foolish. As the serpent spoke, the man entertained those destructive thoughts and would eventually consider the words of the serpent equally as great, or more trustworthy, than those of God. Perhaps the proposition of the serpent was so appealing to Adam and his wife that the words of the Almighty became benign in comparison to the great possibility that they, as a result of eating the forbidden fruit, might "become like God." Whatever the case may be, Adam's thoughts strayed from truth to falsehood, from goodness to evil, from obedience to folly. He allowed his curious nature to betray him, and we feel the rippling effects of his thinking today.

Man's progress (both spiritual and material) is indivisible from his thought: the one will *always* affect the other. He will be a slave to whatever thoughts or ideas have mastered his soul. Adam's thoughts betrayed him, and our thoughts often do the same. Whichever things we have stored up in our hearts, be they positive or negative, will inevitably seep out and make contact with our lives.

If we entertain proper thoughts about the Divine, we are led to salvation and love. If we do not, we follow the crooked and wide path that is so common today. We need not worry about the path getting too crowded, the road is wide and there is plenty of room to roam, but where it leads is the most horrible and pitiful thing about it. Many who walk that road look happy enough, but they walk blindly, following the masses like frightened cattle running for safety, but not really knowing the dangerous gulf that lies at the end of the path.

For this reason, Jesus warned us all by saying: "Enter through the narrow gate. For wide is the road that leads to destruction, and many enter through it. But small is the gate and narrow the road that leads to life, and only a few find it."[66] We should be careful of sweeping and grand spiritual movements that enchant the masses of the world today. It is more likely they are leading us in a direction we ought not to be going. God's real people are holy, and not necessarily popular.

But God has given us a spiritual map in His self-revelation through Scripture to help us avoid that danger, by which we may judge our thoughts about the Divine Mystery and discover which path truly leads to Heaven. We should do our best to allow proper thoughts about our Creator to enter the deepest portions of our souls, and then progress might come as His glory seeps out of our hearts, and gives life to all it touches.

It is true that God is veiled in the darkness of mystery and the glory of His divine love is hidden behind a brilliant light that our minds cannot dim, but He can still be known to us. To illustrate, imagine that for some reason you were walking out in the forest in the middle of the night. And perhaps you run across a camper from some other area, he flashes his light in your face and the light is so shocking to your senses, and so bright, you cannot see behind it. It blinds you and obscures your vision. Then he turns off his bright light and you are now in the dark, still unable to see him because of the problems that darkness cause creatures of the day. But the more time you spent with that person, talking with them and fixing your eyes to see them, they would begin to appear before your eyes. You would slowly begin to see them more clearly. And this is true of how we relate to the Divine. He longs to reveal Himself and establish a relationship with those who reverence His Name.[67] Through His prophet Malachi, He articulates the value He places in souls that convey truth in regard to His revealed nature and character:

> Then those who feared the LORD talked with each other, and the LORD listened and heard. A scroll of remembrance was written in his presence concerning those who feared the LORD and honored his name. 'They will be mine,' says the LORD Almighty, 'in the day when I make up my treasured possession...you will again see the distinction between the righteous and the wicked, between those who serve God and those who do not.'[68]

To open and humble hearts, He delights in the unfolding revelation of His nature and ways, but like so many others before us, we have "rejected knowledge" and because of this, our hearts and souls are not safe. When the bright light shone in the wilderness we turned away from the stranger. We did not want to approach him, even though he presented his presence with the light.

Mankind has a wonderful, spiritual heritage, but most of us are heading in a terrible and foolish direction as we search for satisfaction and spiritual knowledge apart from the Most High God. We are ignoring His heavenly beacon and instead are following disgraceful and shameful things. We have exchanged the truth of God for a lie and are encouraging others to follow suit,[69] forgetting that God will one day call us all to account for our spiritual decisions, and afterwards, He will set aside a people for Himself who would not settle for counterfeit religion.

The truth about God is preached all over the world, in every country known to man. We know the knowledge is available to everyone, because even the Scriptures say, "what may be known about God is plain to them, because God has made it plain to them"[70] through the wonders of His creation.

Unfortunately, "The man without the Spirit does not accept the things that come from the Spirit of God, for they are foolishness to him, and he cannot understand them, because they are spiritually discerned."[71] While God wants to reveal Himself to all of us, in a deeper and more meaningful way than the general revelation of nature, the deep and hidden things of His kingdom can only be penetrated by a humble heart escorted behind the veil of mystery by the Spirit from Heaven. Exclusivity is His divine right, a privilege afforded to Him by the fact that He created all things by His powerful Word. Suffice it to say, we need God to reveal His love and His nature to us. Without His beneficent Spirit working to reveal the greater mysteries of godliness, we will remain terribly uninformed and unenlightened.

The positive progression of our human experience, whether or not we come to enjoy the love of God for ourselves in increasing degree, is dependent upon the working of the Holy Spirit in our thoughts and in our hearts.[72]

> The Spirit searches all things, even the deep things of God. For who among men knows the thoughts of a man except the man's spirit within him? In the same way no one knows the thoughts of God except the Spirit of God. We have not received the spirit of the world but the Spirit who is from God, that we may understand what God has freely given us.[73]

The significance of thought is discerned in the New Testament where Paul tells us in Romans to "be transformed by the renewing of your mind." Further, in Ephesians to "be made new in the attitude of your minds." Accordingly, he repeats the idea in 2 Corinthians when he tells the believing one to "take captive every thought to make it obedient to Christ." Then in Philippians He tells us that "whatever is true, whatever is noble, whatever is right, whatever is pure, whatever is lovely, whatever is admirable—if anything is excellent or praiseworthy—think about such things." Therefore, we must set our hearts and thoughts on things above,[74] and realize that it is only God's Spirit working within that will make our thoughts virtuous and give us the insight that we so greatly need.

Thomas Aquinas said, "the ultimate human glory or happiness lies in nothing else than in knowledge of God."[75] Indeed, "eternal life" is knowing God as He truly is, and living life in light of that fact. The mind of man cannot reach the unattainable God, but in tender love, He might stoop down by His Holy Spirit, and illuminate our hearts. We need knowledge gifted to us from above,[76] as it was to Peter, and when the knowledge is sent, we must receive it gladly. Sadly, like the priests of God who prostituted themselves to false idols, in revelry and sin, many of us have exchanged the truth of God for disgraceful and shameful things.[77]

Nevertheless, Christianity is a mystical and vibrant tradition. Those who devoted themselves to its teachings, and refused to exchange its truth, were met on their journey by the Spirit of God. When He offered His hand to grant them entry through the small gate, they gladly received it. In a manner of speaking, they were taken from this world and seated in Heaven. They were ushered into God's presence and rested in a place where only faithful and meek hearts are able to go. They traveled down a narrow path, and at the end of that road, they were gathered together with a faithful remnant of saints to become His treasured possession.

"To whom will you compare me or count me equal? To whom will you liken me that we may be compared?...Remember this, fix it in mind, take it to heart, you rebels...I am God, and there is no other; I am God, and there is none like me." Isaiah 46:5-9

THE LIGHT WAS GOOD

THOUGHTS ON THE LAND OF DEEPEST NIGHT AND THE GREAT LIGHT OF THE WORLD

"In the beginning God created the heavens and the earth. Now the earth was formless and empty, darkness was over the surface of the deep, and the Spirit of God was hovering over the waters. And God said, 'Let there be light,' and there was light."
Genesis 1:1-3

Let us imagine ourselves lost during the night and stranded in an unfamiliar place—looking for direction, looking for hope, and afraid because of the present darkness. I think we have all experienced similar moments of terror. The darkness is certainly unsettling, and besides someone we know and trust appearing to comfort us, the thing we would probably look for most is light. Even a glimmer of light would bring with it comfort and joy and direction. Our experience makes a point that our spiritual hearts so often ignore: we need the light.

The Jewish prophet Isaiah foretold that the Great Light of the World would one day come. He wrote out of inspiration, penning words of hope about a coming day: "The people walking in darkness have seen a great light; on those living in the land of the shadow of death a light has dawned."[78] With that Light came comfort, joy, and direction for all who understood they were in darkness, and who would, because of their need, be frightened enough to look.

We have to realize that the Bible is full of metaphors and images which try to express spiritual truths in ways that we can understand, and light is a metaphor that is seen in both the New and the Old Testament. In many cases, the spiritual contrast between light and darkness delineates the difference between righteousness and wickedness, between revelation and confusion, between eternal life and spiritual death.

To illustrate, light represents the illumination that comes from the eternal Presence and darkness represents the dim hopelessness of an existence spent away from God's glorious and infinite love. The light represents the life of God, and the darkness represents the emptiness of living without Him. This helps us understand our state even further. Not only are we trying to find something to satisfy that internal longing, but during our search we are, in a manner of speaking, lost in darkness and we are afraid because we have no idea where to turn, where to walk, or what dangers might lay near us. Some are frozen in uncertainty, afraid to even move toward any

THE LIGHT WAS GOOD

direction, while others move freely, not fearing any danger at all. They are still walking in darkness, mind you, but their fear is set aside due to a blissful ignorance—they have convinced themselves that there can be no danger in the search. Nevertheless, both types of travelers need a light to shine in the darkness if they hope to find their Way.

Before there were any light givers like the sun, the moon, and the stars, there was God bringing light into the darkness. Our lives before this special, spiritual revelation resemble the earth at the dawn of creation: formless and empty, darkness filling the deepest portions of our hearts, and the Spirit of the Lord is present and patient, waiting to bring order and direction to our lives—waiting to reveal the light for which we have so long been searching. Until then, our efforts to understand the significance of the love of God and our need for a divine relationship are like that place Job described as "the land of gloom and deep shadow...the land of deepest night...of deep shadow and disorder, where even the light is like darkness."[79]

Admittedly, there are many things about God that are mysterious, but mystery is not an excuse when it comes to obtaining divine revelation and the true knowledge of the Most High. In love, God is ready to give light to all, but Jesus explains the problem we face to His audience while speaking of Himself:

> Light has come into the world, but men loved darkness instead of light because their deeds were evil. Everyone who does evil hates the light, and will not come into the light for fear that his deeds will be exposed.[80]

So it is not that illumination is not possible or even present, on the contrary, we seem to prefer the present darkness. As long as we remain in our present state we can live without reservation and enjoy whatever we please. No longer do we have to concern ourselves with "right" and "wrong," with morality or immorality. If we remain in the darkness those things do not matter. We do not have to worry about people judging our actions, because everything is done in the dark. All the same, we have come to the precipice of a great opportunity, and we need not find ourselves lost in the darkness any longer. Many people will choose to remain in that grim darkness. The Word of God teaches us this truth, and experience is a definite confirmation of that solemn spiritual neglect. However, for some, when the time is right, when they have shunned the darkness, He speaks again as He did in the beginning. In hopeful love, God says "Let there be light," and a new creation begins. The scale is not as grand as the first, of course, but its significance cannot be matched. A brand new world is birthed when light again invades the darkness. A world birthed by revelation. New life transformed from chaos, where the darkness of our hearts is replaced by the light of mysterious and glorious love. It is a revelation that we all need to receive. The prophetic word finds its true fulfillment when we welcome His presence and love—"A light has dawned" in our hearts.

It is similar to finding shelter in the cold darkness of night during that terrible journey and awakening to the rising of the sun. It involves feeling the power of that great star from the heavens warming your face, comforting your soul and living in that moment, not considering anything but beauty and warmth and peace. You awaken to glory and your dark world is transformed into something completely new. You see new horizons and new beauties, where before, all you saw was darkness. That is what revelation is: having your eyes opened to grace, having your heart opened to truth, reaching out and being blessed with knowledge that comes from a Source you cannot touch.

When revelation appears to us, we realize that the divine love is close, that love is all around us. Its light shines down on us and warms every part of our nature. But that is only the beginning. The revelation of love is so provocative that we cannot stop where we began; we long to know it in increasing degree and we want to experience a greater fullness of His surpassing glory.

The true Light that can illuminate the heart and mind of every man has come to show us the way. The Son of God comes and He makes His intentions clear: "I have come into the world as a light, so that no one who believes in me should stay in darkness."[81]

No longer are we doomed to walk blindly through life, but in that blessed morning, when the sun rises for what seems like the very first time, a new voice with new words is heard bursting forth from within our hearts:

> Arise, shine, for your light has come, and the glory of the LORD rises upon you. See, darkness covers the earth and thick darkness is over the peoples, but the LORD rises upon you and his glory appears over you.[82]

When revelation comes, the new creation begins. Providence looks down from above on our formless and empty lives, and speaks words of love that cause the glow of Heaven to shine on His creation and give us hope of a bright, new day. When light is separated from darkness, Love steps into our hearts and leads us to a safe, new life. We first pass through the small gate that forces us to let go of the excess of our old lives, and He leads us down the narrow path of holiness to walk in the light of life.

Just as He did in the beginning, God looks down on us with eyes of love and a heart filled with joy and anticipation. We see the King of Glory smiling down at us from His throne in Heaven, and then we remember that at the beginning of His brand new creation "God saw that the light was good."

> "For God, who said, 'Let light shine out of darkness,' made his light shine in our hearts to give us the light of the knowledge of the glory of God in the face of [Jesus] Christ." 2 Corinthians 4:6

TRUSTWORTHY AND TRUE

Thoughts on Human Faith and the Faithfulness of God

"I will sing of the LORD's great love forever; with my mouth I will make your faithfulness known through all generations. I will declare that your love stands firm forever, that you established your faithfulness in heaven itself." Psalm 89:1-2

To have someone's love for you expressed with words is an experience worth appreciating. All across the globe, "love" is spoken of quite often. Our stores are filled with greeting cards ready with words by which we might express our love and adoration for those closest to us. A great number of the cards are filled with the thought-provoking words of great poets and philosophers who recognized how important love was to the human experience, and then penned heartfelt words to share their insight with the rest of mankind. These cards can be comforting, and certainly have wonderful potential to make their marks within the human soul. But what most will admit is that to merely *speak* of their love is only a superficial offering; we all desire something far more valuable.

With endearing words, many have professed their love for a mate and followed up that declaration of passion with actions that do not befit a devoted partner, spouse, or friend. How many single mothers have an old Valentines' Day card from a former lover and friend who abandoned them when times got tough? Or how many wives have a collection of love letters given them from unfaithful husbands? And even still, how many girlfriends have so recently heard their boyfriends speak of their love for them, only to express the true character of that ephemeral love with mental or physical abuse?

Now, it should be pointed out that although I have used the circumstances of women to clarify my thoughts, we should know that empty declarations of love are spoken by both sexes. Unfaithfulness is an attribute of both men and women. Even men have suffered at the hands of women who declared their love, only to later trample the hearts of the ones they claimed to cherish and adore. Their fragile love was exposed for what it was by the actions and the results that it produced. The character of their love was corrupt. When difficult times came, it could not withstand the pressures of the world. We saw the signs, and could have avoided the danger altogether, but we pitiful humans are always so hopeful.

It is a wonderful curse, this hopefulness. I only call it a curse because though it keeps our hearts open to the possibility that things will be different, too often we approach the situation with blind eyes and unguarded hearts, hoping, always hoping that the next time the love will be real. By real, they are hoping that it will remain faithful and true, hoping that it will be strong enough to withstand the temptations and the adversities of the world. So, we ignore the things that appear to be telling us that this time is no different from before, because we humans are pitifully hopeful creatures.

Yet, faithfulness is a rare quality. The words of the old king are sure: "Many a man claims to have unfailing love, but a faithful man, who can find?"[83] Faithfulness relates to reliability and trustworthiness: if you are faithful, you can be trusted and you are a person many can depend on. We might ask a lover to remain faithful in a relationship, and when we do, we are indicating to them that we want to be able to trust them, we want their heart to remain committed to us and we will appreciate the quality of relationship that comes as a result of that heartfelt devotion.

The faith of the Biblical patriarchs and the testimony of their willingness to follow hard after God meant that they not only knew Him but that they had learned, by His actions, that He could be trusted—He was someone they could depend on. The same testimony can be ours as well. All His words and promises are reliable, and we can safely commit our lives to Him, resting peacefully in the comfort and commitment of His love. Like a bride engaged to be married, in the same way, we cannot and we should not trust our lives to our future Partner unless we can trust Him to be faithful.

The most secure relationships that exist are those in which a person has come to know the character of their mate. If we have carefully judged our companions to be faithful based on our experiences with them, then our hearts are able to rest peacefully in their care. Without this trust, however, our relationship is doomed.

It is fine, then, to ask the question believers throughout the centuries have had to answer. "Can God be trusted?" Truly, if we are to grow in our faith and spirituality, it is the paramount question that we must all answer. To answer this question in the positive moves us toward a new, more fulfilling spiritual experience. To answer in the negative moves us away from our nearest hope. We certainly have enough information available to grant us the appropriate answer, but we do not all come to the same conclusion.

To answer the question correctly, we have to understand the essence of faith. In one regard, "faith is being sure of what we hope for and certain of what we do not see. This is what the ancients were commended for."[84] Words like hope, surety, and certainty are all synonymous with "faith."

I have learned—in contrast to some simple ideas of faith found today—that true Biblical faith has more to do with an *object* than it does a particular *effect*. Effects are important and are often signs of God's activity in our lives and His honoring of our requests, but by object I am referring to that in which we have placed our trust. It is fine to believe and hope for certain things, as we are so accustomed to doing, especially when God has spoken those things to our hearts and challenged us to believe for them, just as He spoke promises to Abraham, Isaac, and Jacob.

Today, though, most people use "faith" as a force and a means by which to satiate all different kinds of hollow and selfish desires. They sanctify those vain hopes by saying, "I'm believing God for this," when so sadly, God has not spoken. They are not things God has placed on the hearts of His people; they are things that our covetous culture polluted our desire and ambition with long ago.

The Kingdom of Heaven is no longer the first thing that we are seeking. We take our ambition and our selfish desire, and try to wash it, cleanse it, and sanctify it, hoping we can take it into the temple where God dwells, praying to no avail, hoping He will use it for His glory. The promise spoken by Jesus that those who abide in Him will have their prayers answered was delivered in light of God's desire to touch the world through His children.[85] Today, we have taken this glorious privilege, and stripped it of its beauty. As Andrew Murray said, "The promise is given in direct connection with the fruitbearing. Limit it to yourself and your own needs, and you rob it of its power."[86] Even still, we forgot the requirement needed to obtain the power of the promise. We are not abiding in Christ. We are children of the world, who abide in its comforts and in its pleasures, rather than the comforts and the pleasures of Heaven.

Faith is far more than merely believing for certain material possessions or situational outcomes (though it can be connected to that), but above all, faith lies in the contentment to allow God to reign in our lives. Faith places the desires and the intentions of God in front of our own—in fact, above our own—and it carries us forward in life when things do not turn out the way we expect, as is often the case. It reminds us that we do not always and we cannot always know what is best. In the midst of our disappointment, it sends us to the Word of Heaven and encourages us to "Trust in the LORD with all your heart and lean not on your own understanding."[87] It is content to allow God to work His goodness on our behalf in ways that He sees fit; it acknowledges the glorious truth that He alone can be trusted. This meekness is what the ancients were commended for. They placed their hope and trust in Christ and in the promise that God would be faithful to them. Because He could be trusted, His promise would always come in His ways and in His time.

A boldness that is not tempered by meekness before God, and a humble submission to His will, is no more than foolish presumption. This is not to say that God does not encourage boldness and confidence in His children, especially when it comes to praying in faith, but the boldest of believers are those who have learned to bow their hearts before God, who have chosen to submit themselves to His working and His power in their lives, and who have discovered the necessity of abiding in Christ for their fruit, power, and growth. The source of sanctified spiritual power is not the saint, it is God who works all and who imparts authority and power to the meek.

But today's idea of faith has been reduced to a science: "If I can believe for _____, then my faith will get it to me" or "If I do X, then Y will happen." However, this methodical approach to spirituality is a very shallow understanding of genuine faith in God. A heart of faith, in essence, says "I surrender my life to you God."

It is one thing to not believe or to not understand that God has the ability to work all things on our behalf, and that He is willing to act favorably toward us in love and grace. It is an entirely different thing to affirm in our hearts that God can truly do all things, that nothing is impossible for Him, and that we have permission to ask anything in the name of Christ since it is His will that we bear much fruit and bring glory to the Father. Then, with all that blessed knowledge we say, "Have your way in my life, Father. I surrender to you." The bravest Christians are those who have truly offered their entire lives to God. Only brave souls can trust Him in this manner. Christ surrendered His life to the cross, and we are called to surrender our lives to Him.

Unfortunately, we have an inner tendency to maintain dominion over our lives. Only when we learn to trust Him completely and totally, can we surrender ourselves to Him fully, as brave souls, resting in the comfort of His everlasting faithfulness.

Abram's story shows us a more trustworthy perspective on faith. God called Abram from the land of his fathers, promised him great things, and worked in His timing to fulfill those things promised. Yet, Abram is not considered "the father of all who believe" because he chose a goal for his future and had the faith to see it come to pass. Instead, he is considered righteous because he "believed God." At the prompting of God Most High, Abram established some goals for his future and He trusted God to fulfill the promises He spoke to him—this is a more trustworthy idea of faith.

Our religious and spiritual culture today, for the most part, is so secular and shallow that it usually thinks that letting God set our goals for us is lazy, and waiting to get God's direction is passivity. This lax religious culture favors proactivity and the drive toward "success," or at least what the world defines as "success." But James used far wiser words when He said:

> Now listen, you who say, 'Today or tomorrow we will go to this or that city, spend a year there, carry on business and make money.' Why, you do not even know what will happen tomorrow. What is your life? You are a mist that appears for a little while and then vanishes. Instead, you ought to say, 'If it is the Lord's will, we will live and do this or that.' As it is, you boast and brag. All such boasting is evil.[88]

It is more blessed to allow God to reign in our lives and to find His hopes, plans, and desires for us, and then to exert the effort of our devotion and trust toward accomplishing those things. Indeed, faith takes effort. We can only trust God to the degree that we know Him, and getting to know God takes time and effort. When we trust in what He says, we can be confident those things will come to pass. But this is why so many of the things today we are hoping for go unfulfilled. It is not generally from a lack of faith, but rather, from our presumption to think that if we simply have "enough faith," whatever we believe will come to pass. The proverbs swiftly correct that foolishness if we are humble enough to heed their words: "In his heart a man plans his course, but the LORD determines his steps."[89] God is willing to speak and set goals for us, but we need to be more diligent in searching out *His* desires, because at the end of the matter, God is in control.

The one who has genuine faith answers that earlier question with wonderful assurance. If they were asked, "Can God be trusted?" They would quickly respond with a "Yes!" The record of God's dealings with mankind as recorded in Scripture and history allows us to judge the matter for ourselves. So, to say that we trust God is essentially the same as saying we have "faith." It is not blind belief or the influence of sincere desire over our rational thinking; it is not hope in something or someone that cannot be identified. No, God is not foolish enough to leave us to our own thinking or reasoning alone. He has given us evidence that we can apprehend, and the evidence of His character moves us to place our trust in Him, as careful souls pondering a future relationship, not wanting to be injured by an unfaithful partner.

Our faith is not strong because of a particularly potent ability to believe, but it is strong because the God in whom we have placed our confidence is mighty in power and faithful to keep His Word.

Yet, when Solomon tells his readers to "Trust in the Lord with all your heart," I think we do not take his words very seriously. Most of us will probably admit that we feel far more comfortable trusting in ourselves. We are afraid we will be disappointed if we trust our hearts to someone we barely know. A sensible person would have a great problem trusting a stranger to do anything, let alone trusting them to take care of important issues in their lives. But this is one of the reasons why God's "name" is so important to us. He cares about who we think He is because if we do not know His character, we will not be able to trust Him. David, King of Israel, confirms this idea when he declares of the Most High: "Those who know your name will trust in you, for you, LORD, have never forsaken those who seek you."[90]

We need to know God's identity, and until we know Him, we cannot trust Him. In our relationships, the wisest advice is that which encourages us to "take some time to get to know the person." In the same way, we must take the time to get to know the Lord. And no matter the spiritual traditions to which we ascribe, we must look critically at their philosophies and their fruit, to see if these traditions can be trusted. We must make sure that the God they promote is "the God and Father of our Lord Jesus Christ," who will, if we believe in His promises, "bless us in the heavenly realms with every spiritual blessing in Christ."[91] Not all the "gods" that different traditions worship are the same, and the Scripture points to our Maker's true identity with its inspired words.

When God appeared to Moses in the form of a burning bush, He declared that He had heard the plight of His people, Israel, and was commissioning Moses to be His messenger. But Moses said to God, "Who am I, that I should go to Pharaoh and bring the Israelites out of Egypt?" God replied to his inquiry by saying, "I will be with you," and He promised a sign that would confirm His presence and power. But then Moses also said to God:

> Suppose I go to the Israelites and say to them, 'The God of your fathers has sent me to you,' and they ask me, 'What is his name?' Then what shall I tell them?" God said to Moses, "I am who I am. This is what you are to say to the Israelites: 'I AM has sent me to you'...'The Lord, the God of your fathers—the God of Abraham, the God of Isaac and the God of Jacob—has sent me to you.' This is my name forever, the name by which I am to be remembered from generation to generation.[92]

Now in the ancient world, names used to hold great significance. A man's name was one of His most coveted and prized possessions. As Lester Sumrall said, "Often a name provides an important clue to the nature of a person or place...The Bible refers to God by many different names, and each one reveals some aspect of God's character or His relationship with us."[93]

If God had not revealed His name to Moses, the people of Israel would have had no reason to trust that he was truly His emissary, and that their time of suffering would soon end. But because God sent His name with Him, the people could identify who was working on their behalf, and were then obliged to trust that their deliverance was sure. They had heard the stories of His faithfulness as we hear them today. They remembered the great "I AM," the God of their fathers, and because they knew who He was, they knew they could trust He and Moses to be faithful. They remembered the One who established them in the earth, and were certainly reminded of the promise of deliverance He made long before.

Even today, God wants us to know how important His "name" is—not the word in particular that we use—but the truth, the character, and the identity which belies the extreme significance of the word. Names are important only because quite often names denote different identities, however, sometimes a similar use of names can cause more confusion than clarity. The *Allah* of Mohammed is not the *Father* of Jesus. In the same respect, the *Father* of orthodox Christians is different from the *Father* of Mormons; the *Jehovah* of Christians is fundamentally different from the *Jehovah* of Jehovah's Witnesses.

We might say the Muslims, the Hindus, the Mormons, and the Jehovah's Witnesses worship something they call god, but their idea of God is different from that of the Christian. The names Muslims and Hindus ascribe to their deity bear witness to that fact, while Mormons and Jehovah's Witnesses use the same names as that of Christians, while pouring into those names some duplicitous and deluded information. Their gods might share some similar characteristics, and in the case of Jehovah's Witnesses and Mormons, even the same names, but each attribute that the Christian affirms is so great and so vital to the nature of God, that the moment an attribute is removed from our conception of the Creator, He is no longer the same divine Personality, but His identity is changed into something inglorious.

When we say names are important, we mean really "identities," and not so much the actual words. The Christian hopes and trusts in their magnificent Father because His nature, devotion, and character are unchanging. They have identified Him by His Word and His activity in their lives. They know who He is, and who He will remain, always resting in the confidence that they serve "the Father of the heavenly lights who does not change like shifting shadows,"[94] and not the gods of those previously mentioned religious sects.

The immutable character of God is an encouraging landmark in our search for spiritual truth. The divine love, like God Himself, cannot change; if it could, it would cease to be divine. Therefore, only God's love can be trusted to remain faithful to us. We humans are hopeful creatures. But we certainly have reason to hope. The psalmist declared that God's love "stands firm forever."[95] There is no degree of change within His love; He loves us all the same, and that love will never change.

I think that at some point in our lives we have all had to cope with the pain of a broken heart. Our common relationships are all temporal and transitory, subject to time and negative change, and therefore, cannot last with the consistency that we all desire and the faithfulness that we can all trust. We see this with the instability of the human body, the development of the human personality, and even in nature. With time, our bodies morph, our personalities change and become more defined, and the world around us changes every season. Things around us are in constant flux. As such, there are very few things in the world on which we should choose to rely.

Yet we love, and we continue to love, always in the hope that one day we might find a love that does not change. On the one hand, it is a terrible thought, but on the other hand its hopefulness gives us hope. We know there is a love somewhere we can rely on. And despite the discouraging evidence of our failed relationships, we keep looking for that love. Our natural and spiritual hopefulness is not without a positive end. If it is truly a curse, it is only a blessed one, because we do have reason to hope.

The instability of human love can be dangerous if its object is allowed to ascend to the throne of our hearts. We usually allow that object to ascend in our hearts because there is a reciprocation of love that we are trusting and hoping will remain. But since human love is transitory, when the ruler of our hearts rebukes us or betrays the trust we have placed in them, we often crumble in disappointment because of the power we have given that person. This unjust and unfaithful ruler can destroy their new kingdom as he or she wills, with no regard for our hearts or lives. Their only concern is for themselves.

The throne of our hearts holds great power. We must be careful to whom we defer lordship, and to whom we commit our love and our faith. If we rely only on our emotional bearings and forget to consult our dear friends wisdom, discernment, Scripture, and Spirit, we will certainly choose a ruler who cannot be trusted. However, if we consult our righteous companions, they will encourage us to take the time to look critically at the possible ruler's character, to discover whether or not they can be trusted with our hearts.

It is the nature of man to search out and hope for something better and greater than that which they know, to look for someone who is faithful in a world where commitment is rare. Unbeknownst to us, we often allow unfaithful stewards to occupy the throne of power within, and to dwell in the place that can only be ruled safely by the One whose heart of love will never change. Consequently, the new rulers disappoint us, time and time again.

Truly, only God can establish a kingdom that lasts forever, and with faithful love brighten our lonely hearts for all time. The world around us may crumble and we might find ourselves at odds with everything we have ever loved when He comes to rule our hearts, but He is a noble King, who will fight for that kingdom, defending His new home with all His might. So we should not give up hope because of our constant failure. There is a Rock on which we can stand for refuge when the waters of an uncertain world come to wash away the sands of our lives from beneath us. We can rest our hearts safely on that Rock and be assured that the troubles and the anxieties of a frantic world cannot move it. God's love remains as a constant and devoted affection in a world that is incurably subject to change.

Many people often search their entire lives for a love that will endure the test of time, a love strong enough to withstand the temptations and the adversities of the world. But the Faithful One, who longs to occupy the throne of our hearts, wants us to know that He can be trusted. He further promises that He will prove the faithfulness of His love to us by what He does in our lives.

As careful hearts should, we ask Him His name. We hear His response as He prepares to take His seat on the throne of our hearts; words of comfort flow from the mouth of the eternal and unchanging God of love as He reveals His holy name. He says, "I am Trustworthy and True."[96]

> "I will betroth you to me forever…I will betroth you in faithfulness, and you will acknowledge the LORD." Hosea 2:19-20

MY PEOPLE

THOUGHTS ON THE WAY TO THE FATHER, THE TRUTH THAT MOST DENY, AND THE LIFE THAT ALL MEN NEED

"See to it that no one takes you captive through hollow and deceptive philosophy, which depends on human tradition and the basic principles of this world rather than on Christ."
Colossians 2:8

I have heard it said before that the goal of religion is to control mankind, and that the fruit of all religion is evil. To some, the harvest of all theological effort is slavery, and the tool by which this deceptive fruit is gathered is fear. If we study the majority of the world's religions, we might find that these accusations are absolutely true. When the fruit of most religious philosophy is gathered, upon close inspection, it is found that the harvest is contaminated and unfit for any to enjoy. The faithful among them toil and labor to feast upon what cannot be earned. They scale heights they are not permitted to scale on their own, and eat fruit from a tree we were all commanded to avoid.

But far from the taint of the aforementioned spiritual fruit lies a Tree of Life, much like the one that dwelt in the middle of the Garden of Eden, the place of perfect peace. The tree is visible to all, but only appealing to a few. Curiosity often gets the best of most, and they choose to eat from the tree with forbidden and corrupted fruit—undeniably, it killed the cat, but in our folly we never think it would do the same to us.

This same curiosity was undoubtedly the gift that led to Pandora's grave mistake. The jar could not open itself. Her curiosity enticed her, and a whole host of evils was unleashed on the world. Like Pandora, we do not control our curiosity with the prudence that would keep our lives from devastation. The wise see danger and take refuge, but we tend to keep going and suffer for it.[97]

Nevertheless, the fruit from that dangerous tree does look appealing, and it seems to be useful for gaining knowledge. Many testify to the benefits of its fruit, though they have not truly taken the time to inspect it critically. So they feast, refusing to heed the warning given so long ago that its fruit leads to death, encouraging others to eat along with them. They satisfy their curiosity, all at the cost of their souls.

The other tree, in stark contrast to the deceptive one, is untainted by perversion or corruption, and its fruit is profitable for all.[98] In a manner of speaking, its roots are now fixed on the summit of a holy mount we call Zion. Its sanctified ground is not unlike that on which Moses stood when He ascended to gain audience with the Lord during the Exodus out of Egypt. Fortunately, there are those who are permitted to scale its heights and dine on the fruit of the Divine. But only God knows the Way, and only He can grant us entry through the small gate, which leads to the narrow and blessed path. This is why He sent His Son. Because His body is the gate and His words are the path, and He is able to show us the Way. If we follow the direction of His living Word, we too may ascend to the heights of Jehovah, and share in the fellowship of love divine.

Historical revision, as well as the ignorance and the memory of recent human history casts a dim light on what the general population knows of the teachings of Jesus and the Church He established with His blood. In almost every generation, we can find evidence of perverters of the Christian religion who used the banner of Christ as a means by which to justify all types of evil. It has caused many adherents to the Christian faith to expel the word *religion* from their entire vocabulary, as if the word itself carries with it some wicked connotation.

The fact of the matter is that the Christian faith *is* a religion. The means of this religion are different from all others, though, and the aim is definitely unique. Its faithful approach God on the path that they believe He has lain before us all, as opposed to reasoning which way they think God might more likely be reached. This was the mistake of Saul, the first king of Israel, when he tried to honor the Lord through disobedience, without regard for His command.[99] This was the folly of Adam and Eve in the Garden, as they did not consider the warning of the Lord true, and tasted immediate spiritual death, with the physical form to come later, as they were separated from the original Tree of Life.[100] This is the confusion that we see today as men and women "gather around them a great number of teachers to say what their itching ears want to hear," as we try our best to honor God in a way that we see fit, to gain an audience with the Lord Most High on the sacred ground of His holy mountain.[101]

We make this sad mistake not realizing that Jehovah has paved a way for His treasured possession, a narrow and small path that the saints have named "Holiness." We inspect the mountain, looking for a clear trail ourselves, not wanting to restrict ourselves to that despised and rejected path. We look for a way that will lead us to the top with as little effort as possible—certainly one where we are able to avoid as much physical discomfort as we can. We do not want to reject our old ways, or our old passions, and we think we see plenty of ways to make it on our own terms. However, if we would find that new Tree of Life, the communion of love everlasting, we must choose to forsake all other paths and follow God's direction alone. The paths may appear to be going in the same direction, but I promise you, they are not headed toward the same place.

One thinker said it like this:

> Human beings as a lot are incurably religious. The problem is that since these same human beings are also infected by sin, they tend not to desire to honor and glorify the true God, who is righteous and holy. Rather, they tend to make gods for themselves that are pleasing to them or that satisfy some sense of what they think a god ought to be. As John Calvin said, the human mind is a factory for idols. Such gods, concocted by the rationale of humans apart from special revelation, are invariably out of touch with the truth.[102]

The sacred Scriptures tells us that the problem persists not from a lack of knowledge, but by man's willingness to reject divine revelation, and their desire to create gods that appeal to their frail and imperfect nature;[103] we let them guide us into folly time and time again, and have exchanged the glory of the immortal God for inglorious pursuits.

It does not matter how much truth is preached if all we ever do is pick and choose and never experience the blessing of divine revelation. Truth without revelation cannot lead us to regeneration. To transform a dead soul, Truth and Revelation must meet at the altar of faith, hope and love. The excited couple must exchange vows before God and commit to each other in an eternal union that neither time nor the world can dissolve. To see genuine spiritual blessing, they cannot live apart. There is no new life and no sanctified union, without the presence of them both.

The world is full of so-called Christians who acknowledge Truth and claim her as a daughter, but when the important moment comes they will never agree to give her to her rightful husband, Revelation. They deny that union at their own peril, refusing to admit that divine Truth only loves spiritual Revelation. Our knowledge is useless if it only rests in the head, and is never allowed to touch the heart and transform our lives.

Now, if a religion is "a system of beliefs and practices that express devotion to God,"[104] then the faith of those who follow the teachings of Jesus is certainly the definitive expression of *true religion*. It is the Way that God has declared, by which His faithful ones may express their devotion to their Sovereign Lord, it is the blessed union of truth and revelation, and the cultivation of a divine relationship shared between creature and Creator.

Religion is by no means the aim of the Christian's spiritual form, discipline and perseverance, but it is the framework that God has presented; the "blueprint" through which we all might be "built up to become a dwelling in which God lives by His Spirit."[105] The implication found in these words, then, is that as we are in ourselves, we are not fit to house the glory of God. Our sin's sickness separates us from that holy habitation and constant communion, but *His* religion shows us how we might enjoy that everlasting newness of life and love. It shows how we can prepare ourselves to be God's "dwelling"—the place where He abides. So true religion is what leads us to a proper relationship with God. You cannot have the latter without first receiving the former. It is the objective measuring rod by which we may guide our spiritual progress and learn how we might properly worship our wonderful Maker.

Without this true religion, our spiritual efforts would be just as fruitless as all the other religious and spiritual movements that were inspired by the impetus of a "very spiritual," yet very subjective experience. We would wander aimlessly, each heart in its own direction, following excitement and euphoria, but none would take a single step toward God—the true ecstasy.

He must be careful with us, our God of love, for we are like sheep, and sheep are known to be quite foolish. Even so, true religion cannot earn us an audience with the Lord of creation, and neither can it repay Him for everything He has already done. It cannot help us gain access to our heavenly Home on the grounds of merit; it merely reveals to us the fact that He has blazed a trail to eternal life for a remnant He has set apart for Himself. He has given those believers a careful map to follow in His written Word. By heeding its direction, they can reach the summit of Salvation. Their hearts can ascend to their true Home, where satisfaction, peace and love are. True religion, therefore, is not only important, it is necessary for us all.

In the book of James we are told that, "Religion that God our Father accepts as pure and faultless is this: to look after orphans and widows in their distress and to keep oneself from being polluted by the world."[106] I wonder, then, if God Himself does not have an aversion to the use of the word "religion," why do we? He does not use the word an extraordinary number of times, but in its use, it is connected to loving and good will toward men, holiness, and purification from evil— virtues that most today claim to hold in high esteem. The words of the old preacher serve to correct our foolish thinking:

Religion is meant to be in everyday life a thing of unspeakable joy. And why do so many complain that it is not so? Because they do not believe that there is no joy like the joy of abiding in Christ and in His love, and being branches through whom He can pour out His love on a dying world.[107]

But in times such as these, saying that Christianity is a religion within some Christian circles is taboo. Perhaps it is that some do not know what true religion is, and they fear that our faith, our devotion, and our worship will be lumped together with that tainted crop of "spiritual" fruit we see today and tossed away as it all should be. So they have become afraid of what religion means to the world and have tried to expel it from their vocabulary and our culture without first discovering for themselves what true religion means to us all.

The fear is understandable considering the cultural mood of the day, but Christianity is not a metamorphic set of beliefs and ideals; it is a sanctified trust in the Creator, a holy way of living in a common world, a glorious ideal that we cannot attain on our own, a gracious proclamation of goodness, and the love of God being poured into human hearts. Our religion is sacred, and although the world might not appreciate it as such, its simplest teachings have never and can never change. We have a holy heritage that cannot be denied, truth that we must defend for the sake of all mankind.

James' quote about pure and faultless religion seems a little vague, and given the language used, it seems that it could leave a possibility for many religions to fall under this category of "pure and faultless," leaving us at a strange and confusing crossroads in our thinking about true religion.

But this section of James' very passionate letter was perhaps referring to a host of Old Testament Scriptures, among which is Isaiah chapter 1, wherein God rebukes the Israelites for the way they perverted His holy decrees: "wash and make yourselves clean. Take your evil deeds out of my sight! Stop doing what is wrong, learn to do what is right! Seek justice, encourage the oppressed. Defend the cause of the fatherless, plead the case of the widow."[108]

Religion of the heart is indeed what God desires; a religion where inward transformation takes place and replaces hollow philosophy and empty form; where a relationship with the Source of the divine love is cultivated and nurtured; thankfully, God has placed a spiritual beacon in the world by which we might find His true religion. He has given us an objective form that leads us to subjective and holy experience, to purification and sincere worship.

Certainly, we can spot virtue in many different traditions. In some it is definitely easier to spot than in others. C.S. Lewis made the following statement, and by his words he shed light on a very tender subject:

> If you are a Christian you do not have to believe that all the other religions are simply wrong all through…If you are a Christian, you are free to think that all those religions, even the queerest ones, contain at least some hint of truth…But of course, being a Christian does mean thinking that where Christianity differs from other religions, Christianity is right and they are wrong. As in arithmetic—there is only one right answer to a sum, and all other answers are wrong; but some of the wrong answers are much nearer being right than others.[109]

The proper answers to our spiritual inquiries are the most important matter. The effort put forth to pursue this knowledge is not particularly considered. If your conclusion is incorrect, it shows that all your effort was in vain.

I am sure that God was speaking to men all over the world, while holding out virtue to those who were willing to listen. However, nowhere else do we find a love as comprehensive and as perfect as that of Christ, a philosophy as healthy as that found in the teachings of The Way. Its words do not promise a perfect life, but they do promise a perfect end. They promise that one day, if we adhere to its message of repentance and allow God to change our hearts and lives, we will see His face and behold Him in glory.¹¹⁰ They do promise love, joy, peace, patience, kindness, goodness, faithfulness, gentleness and self-control.¹¹¹ This is the spiritual fruit that Jesus Christ promises us through His Spirit, when we turn from the sinful life. The fruit comes only from the Tree of Life, and only Jesus can lead us up the mount, to the peak of Zion, to enjoy the fruit of love divine.

> Jesus Christ is the Son of God's love, the Bearer, the Bringer, the Dispenser of love. What God is as invisible in heaven, He was as visible on earth. He came, He lived, He suffered and died only to glorify the Father—that is, to let it be seen how glorious the Father in His love is, and to show that in the Godhead there is no other purpose than to bless men and make them happy; to make it manifest that the highest honor and blessedness of any being is to give and to sacrifice.¹¹²

For this reason, the Scriptures testify to the greatness of this same Jesus. They shout across time and space, encouraging us to believe their report:

> He is the image of the invisible God, the firstborn over all creation. For by him all things were created: things in heaven and on earth, visible and invisible, whether thrones or powers or rulers or authorities; all things were created by him and for him. He is before all things, and in him all things hold together. And he is the head of the body, the church; he is the beginning and the firstborn from among the dead, so that in everything he might have the supremacy. For God was pleased to have all his fullness dwell in him, and through him to reconcile to himself all things, whether things on earth or things in heaven, by making peace through his blood, shed on the cross.¹¹³

Without a doubt, the evidence of history speaks to the power of the love of this same Jesus as well. The words of that late Civil Rights leader, who lost his life as a martyr for the cause of equality, shortly after God—through the Spirit perhaps—took him "to the mountaintop" to look over at the promised future of his people, speak to the veracity of Christ's Lordship: "Evil may so shape events that Caesar will occupy a palace and Christ a cross, but one day that same Christ will rise up and split history into A.D. and B.C., so that even the life of Caesar must be dated by his name."[114] There will never be another spiritual Teacher whose words transcend the impediment of time as Jesus' words do still; there is power in His name that no other name can hold. He not only taught us of love, but He showed it in a way that no one else can, and He left this earth so that by His eternal Spirit that same love might be poured into our hearts.[115]

Because of this glorious fact, Christianity is the measuring rod of righteousness, peace, truth and love. The further we deviate from its message, the hollower our religious ideals are seen to be. The more we emulate it, the greater it becomes. This is why alternative religions that share virtues in common with Christianity can look appealing and confusing at the same time. Divine truth is not a commodity that only Christians control. We are said to be "stewards of the secret things of God," but spiritual revelation is the gift of God to humanity, and He offers His insight to all who will receive it.

One of the second century Christian apologists, Justin Martyr, in writing to the rulers of the Roman Empire during his day, was said to have portrayed a similar idea. A contemporary theologian summarizes that idea with these words:

> Traces of truth that may be discovered in pagan philosophers' writing before Christ were borrowed from the Hebrew Scriptures or else are due to the pre-incarnate Christ as Logos (the rational power guiding the universe) enlightening them.[116]

There is something in our thinking that limits the activity of God to the Holy Land. It is most likely our very simple and small idea of God that limits His presence and love to a particular region of our world. Assuredly, His activities there long ago were those He chose to have recorded for our benefit.

In that regard, that land is absolutely holy. But the Scriptures tell us that "The earth is the LORD's and everything in it, the world, and all who live in it...."[117] God's domain, then, is much bigger than a particular region of our planet. So, it is not implausible or heretical to say that God was speaking all over the world to special souls who would listen and respond to truth, preparing them for the blessed Hope of Jesus Christ, who would appear one day in Israel and tell mankind to "Repent, for the kingdom of heaven in near."[118]

This particular idea might account for the inexplicable appearance in the story of Abraham of the mysterious man and king, Melchizedek, who was said to be "priest of God Most High."[119] Since Abraham's interaction with God was so intimate, in our thinking we might assume that Abraham was the sole vessel through which God was interacting with mankind. Though he was the central figure at the time, and the one through which God had chosen to bless all the nations of the world, we can be sure that he was not the lone individual with which God was communing. Since we do not have record of a holy priesthood established by God until later in the biblical accounts, we can then conclude that Melchizedek's priesthood and knowledge of the Most High God was established in a story and an experience of which we have no account.

We have no inspired and reliable record of God's dealings with men and women throughout the world beyond that of the biblical patriarchs, though some say the pagan myths that share commonalities with the biblical record are perversions of the truth that God was offering to man to prepare them for the coming of His Son. This could account for the flood stories shared in cultures across the globe, as well as other accounts which might mimic the story of man's creation, original sin, and the coming of a divine savior to rescue mankind from some epic danger. Even the story of Pandora, which was alluded to earlier, has its parallels to the Christian idea of original sin, as well as the possibility of a future hope for mankind, not yet experienced—which Christians, of course, have discovered in Jesus Christ.[120]

There is no need to suggest that Christians have stolen these ideas from pagan traditions to build their religious heritage; the similarities are most likely due to God's dealings with mankind as a whole and His desire to impart truth to people throughout the world. Truly, the Scripture makes this idea very possible when it tells us that God "wants all men to be saved and to come to a knowledge of the truth."[121]

The ancient philosophers of antiquity, the noble thinkers of centuries past, the long-gone scientists of enlightenment, and even many today who have never claimed to be Christian, can know and explain certain levels of truth. The Christian should not deny this, they should relish it. It only further enhances the idea that absolutes exist, and that God is revealing those universal truths to the human spirit, holding men, in a "relative" world, accountable for the knowledge they receive from Him, and how they choose to respond.

As has always been the case, humans are notorious for rejecting and distorting divine truth. That being said, we might notice virtue in other traditions besides the one that honors Jesus Christ as Lord. Even so, we attribute that to the grace of God reaching out to man and preserving the world through His goodness. We might also attribute the lack of virtue that pervades the rest to mankind's rejection of complete spiritual virtue. Where virtue is preserved and aggressively upheld, civilization appears far more civilized, but where virtue is denied and distorted, civilization and its people suffer horribly. Virtue is God's holy preservative. It is that which keeps the world from destroying itself completely.

This is why Truth and Revelation must meet together in our hearts, and fall in love. Their offspring is righteous, and can help to preserve our world. Although they cannot change the world completely, since its people, at large, are headed gleefully toward perdition, they can make a tremendous impact and lead others to the wise words of their mother Truth. Unfortunately, if Revelation is rejected and rebuked, then Truth may later be prostituted and manipulated by some unloving suitors. Her children, then, will be unholy, Fatherless, and they will lead the world toward decadence and not toward spiritual life.

Nevertheless, we are like children who refuse to take our vitamins, sad little ones who refuse to eat our vegetables, but the sustenance we are rebuking is spiritual truth, and the accompanying suffering and malnutrition will not be seen in our bodies, it will be borne in our souls.

Since man's expulsion from the perfect Garden of Eden, we have been searching for a way to reenter the Paradise that was lost in the beginning, because only God can lead us to the Tree of Life we spurned so long ago, when we chose to eat fruit from that wicked tree.

On our trek, we sometimes spot that other tree. It still looks appealing too, and the temptation to veer toward it is strong. But when Love is sent to walk before us, in all His divine glory, we must leave all our deluded teachers, spiritual guides, and empty traditions behind and choose to follow Him alone. He says, "Leave them; they are blind guides. If a blind man leads a blind man, both will fall into the pit."[122] And He is not so careless that He tells us to leave our guides and walk alone. Instead Jesus says, "Follow me," "I am The Way." As a welcome consequence, if we are brave enough to follow Him, we will finally taste the fruit of the Tree of Life, and be inhabited and consumed by the fiery passion of God.

If we tread the path that God has put before us, our hearts of stone will be transformed and changed into hearts of love, akin to the purification of which James spoke, which is in fact the goal of true religion. Thankfully, we find that the harvest of the Christian philosophy is liberty and not control, purification and not empty form, and the tool by which this holy fruit is gathered is love divine. Its fruit is charming and safe, leading only to life eternal. Those who have tasted the glory of God know this to be so, and from them this revelation cannot be stolen. There is a "perfect law that gives freedom," and its author is Christ.[123]

On Mount Sinai, when God sanctified Himself in the eyes of Israel, He warned Moses and said "the people must not force their way through to come up to the LORD." The message He conveyed is true even today: God is holy. He expects us to honor His words as such and only approach Him the way He has declared. But His Son lifts the spirits of our disappointed hearts when He says, "I am The Way," and again "Come unto me...I will give you rest." When we realize that apart from our own spiritual fantasies there is a God who longs to be near us, then we will follow His way without foolishly blazing a trail of our own "to come up to the LORD" the way *we* see fit.

Truth matters, as it always has, but today, Truth has been replaced by relativity and confusion, and Love replaced by rebellion and manipulation. Philosophers and theologians quote the words of Jesus when giving some grand insight into spiritual principles, and call Him a liar in the same breath when they say that singular truth does not exist, that there must be more than one Way to God.

Like those spoken of in the book of Jude, "they are godless men, who change the grace of our God into a license for immorality and deny Jesus Christ as our *only* Sovereign and Lord."[124] It is an affront to Jesus' message and to His life. Before He laid down His life for the sake of His love, He told His disciples "I am the *way* and the *truth* and the *life*. No one comes to the Father except through me."[125] Unless we find true religion, and seek the path which has been laid before us, all our efforts to ascend the holy mount where the presence of the Lord dwells will be horribly unsuccessful.

The psalmist, David, asks some interesting questions and then gives a very pertinent response: "Who may ascend the hill of the LORD? Who may stand in his holy place? He who has clean hands and a pure heart, who does not lift up his soul to an idol or swear by what is false. He will receive blessing from the LORD...."[126]

Today's religion, and sadly this includes much of what we think these days to be "Christian," professes to hold things sacred, but refuses to sanctify itself within the boundaries of genuine spiritual truth. Many swear by what is false, and encourage others to take similar oaths, exchanging the glory of Truth for ignoble and impotent gods.

Yet throughout the world, there is a remnant of grace—the followers of The Way are still thriving and growing in love. On mount Zion they worship day and night, and their hearts glow before God like fireflies in the night, as they present themselves before Him with dancing and singing.[127] Their existence is, in a manner of speaking, invisible and mysterious. To some extent, we cannot definitively pinpoint who they are, but God knows His people. The value and the preciousness of their fellowship and love cannot be measured numerically. To God, their worth is spiritual and priceless; their numbers are small in comparison to most religious groups, because God is concerned with quality and not necessarily quantity. He will trade a million base and vile servants for one heart, pure and repentant. He will open the way to life eternal for one heart who asks for grace, mercy and love: for one soul, with clean hands, washed in the waters of repentance.

Sadly, many of us are those of whom Christ spoke centuries ago and we "were not willing" to return to His arms.[128] We love wickedness rather than the truth, and by following the mixed and muddled teachings of the world, we reject the gospel of God. Our religion, then, is only a set of rules taught by men, with no hope to reach the transcendent Creator, and no power to transform our hearts. We have added ritual and neglected adoration and Spirit; hollow and deceptive it is indeed, but we very much prefer it to the truth. We come near to God with our mouths, but our hearts are far from Him.

We want no part in the glorious mystery of God, His Church, nor the purity of true religion. We have exchanged the glory of the immortal God for false hopes; we have exchanged the truth of God for lies, while worshipping and serving created things rather than the Creator.[129] But oh, how our hearts *and His* would rejoice if we would return to Him. We speak of love so longingly, and act as if we want to know it more than anything else. Neglecting the voice of the Divine, we turn our hearts away from our nearest hope. Nonetheless, in love, He is calling, and in hope, He is waiting.

One day soon, perhaps we will begin our search for God, and choose to enter through that small gate the saints call "Repentance," whose handle we call "Faith, Hope, and Love." Maybe we will walk down the narrow path it leads to, which the people of God call "Holiness," and then say to our friends and loved ones that we once led astray, "Come, let us go up to Zion, to the LORD our God."[130]

But what are we to make of those who might say that the way to God has many roads like the paths up a mountain, which all intersect at divine truth? For them, I would have to point back to Mount Sinai, where God established a holy boundary that the people were not to cross. They could not enter His presence or force their way up the mountain on their own, else they would incur His wrath and be destroyed.

The first woman, Eve, was the first to make that sad mistake. She saw that the tree that the Lord had commanded her and her husband not to eat from was "desirable for gaining wisdom," and in disobedience she sought that wisdom apart from God. She transgressed the holy boundary and profaned the Word of the Lord. She forgot that the equation had only one correct answer, and she chose the wrong one.

Today, God's wayward children try their best to forge their own path to Jehovah. They waste their breath trying to scale the heights of that holy hill on their own. There are perhaps hundreds of thousands of religions and philosophies that exist today. Furthermore, they differ to such a great extent that some affirm God as a spirit-being far removed from us and totally detached from what exists, while the opposite extremes insist that no God exists at all and to seek Him is meaningless. Their bastion of truth and life and love lies elsewhere. It is, therefore, dangerously irreverent and horribly misinformed to suggest that all religions lead to the same place, since some point to "God" while others deny God and point to a different hope.

Unless God Himself is confused about the issue, we should not find ourselves stifled by these varying traditions—we are, of course, "incurably religious." "True religion," however, "confronts earth with heaven and brings eternity to bear upon time,"[131] and we can trust our souls to its teaching.

To say that one religion is not sufficient to fulfill the needs of humanity or to account for the souls throughout the world, is to demean the virtue of our religion as well as the character, wisdom, and the sovereignty of the God who has given that religion to us. Undeniably, His dominion is global and His religion can heal us all. What God gives is always effective.

There is an answer to the great problem of our current spiritual misfortunes; there is a way to discover how to begin our journey to the heart of God. When we discover that narrow path, and enter through the small gate, we may, in a manner of speaking, reenter the Garden of Eden from which Adam and Eve were expelled. We may approach the sacred hill the saints call Zion, and ascend its heights toward the Tree of Life. We will find the fruit of life eternal there, and in liberty, enjoy the Most Holy Place. There the saints of God will sing their song, and the angels of Heaven will dance. There lost souls will shout for joy, as God holds them in His hands.

Now His invisible nation is visible. As they stand on Zion singing, with a multitude of other sacred hearts, He appears. This King of Glory, the Lord God strong and mighty, comes to celebrate with them and to deliver a message of grace. His eyes filled with joy, with passion, and with love. The saints stand silent before Him, their eyes welling over with tears of joy waiting for Him to speak. From His mouth come words of power the likes of which they have never felt. They fall to their knees in worship as He claims them for Himself. "I am the LORD your God," He says, "You are my people."[132]

"Therefore, brothers, since we have confidence to enter the Most Holy Place by the blood of Jesus, by a new and living way opened for us through the curtain, that is, his body, and since we have a great priest over the house of God, let us draw near to God with a sincere heart in full assurance of faith, having our hearts sprinkled to cleanse us from a guilty conscience and having our bodies washed with pure water." Hebrews 10:19-22

ALL THINGS EXIST FOR HIM

THOUGHTS ON THE FREEDOM OF MAN AND THE SOVEREIGNTY OF GOD

"As the rain and the snow come down from heaven, and do not return to it without watering the earth and making it bud and flourish, so that it yields seed for the sower and bread for the eater, so is my word that goes out from my mouth: It will not return to me empty, but will accomplish what I desire and achieve the purpose for which I sent it." Isaiah 55:10-11

Our story begins with four inspired and insightful words—"In the beginning God." Without obligation or coercion, without necessity or petition—*God*. A beautiful picture of sovereignty indeed is the fact that before the universe existed God was acting, creating, and preparing. He was making choices freely and independently of our faith or our obedience. The Scripture emphatically declares that we took no part in it, and that He gave us no opportunity to give input. The beginning of the written Word silences all our supposed power and our foolish presumption with four words—"In the beginning God." We will find comfort in our lives if we realize that these words and their meaning have never changed.

Creation was ordered by God, and because of this, everything has a divine purpose: a niche in the plan of Providence. It is not without cause that the Scripture was penned, "The heavens declare the glory of God; the skies proclaim the work of His hands."[133] I think the most beautiful things in our universe have, imbedded within them, the signature of God's creative and sovereign order that continually comforts our souls.

When God formed the earth He divided the light from the darkness, the heavenly from the earthly. He separated man from animal and night from day. He established time and space, and assigned the stars their homes in the heavens. There is order everywhere that cannot be destroyed, for "By the word of the LORD were the heavens made, their starry host by the breath of his mouth...he spoke, and it came to be; he commanded, and it stood firm."[134]

His providential hand even moves in our situations and circumstances. "For the LORD watches over the way of the righteous,"[135] and we can trust our lives to His care. Nothing in our lives is hidden from His sight or His plan, nothing small and nothing great. Everything within creation is subject to the order that God established, and that divine design perpetually produces grace before our eyes. If we discover the design and find our place within its order, we will see its beauty and enjoy its goodness in our lives. But in all honesty, we do not always recognize the order infused into the creation, or into our lives for that matter. It definitely causes us to wonder whether God is truly the Sovereign Lord of the universe and in absolute control of our lives.

We see Earth move, kill, and destroy, and think that Chaos reigns supreme, that Chance is our god, and luck is his seemingly divine power. We see Violence sweep across the globe with all her bloody terror and then wonder why, if there were a divine plan, things seem to be progressing the way they are. Then in our lives, we face disappointment and heartache, dark nights of the soul, and we wonder where things could have gone wrong.

Yet, to be Sovereign Ruler of the universe, God must have all knowledge, all power, and the wisdom necessary to utilize both His knowledge and His power to effectively bring His plans to fruition. Key to this sovereignty is the fact that God must also be free to choose and able to do whatever He deems fit, whatever *He* desires. Thus, God maintains the divine and irrevocable right to rule His creation in any way He chooses.

The sovereignty of God assures us nothing in our lives is out of His control; that there was, and still is, a divine plan for mankind. However, what we have done in our freedom has caused the world to think that there was no plan at all, that the mark left by humanity's continual folly is all there is and ever will be. Nevertheless, Providence is still at work in the world and in the lives of men and women, but the evidence of humanity is not making God's sovereign choices look very wise. Be that as it may, the design of the Creator is not flawed; we just do not see it as clearly as we should. Our choices have shaped and molded the world; it is because of the way we have used our God-given liberty that the world looks the way it does. God is still sovereign, but in His sovereignty, He chose to make us free.

Long ago God decided to form a creature after His own likeness, a created spirit with the unique ability to love. A creature made for *His* divine pleasure. It would be called "Adam,"[136] and he would be given a special and dangerous gift to make it possible for him to love. Adam would be able to make choices. He would have liberty, a quality shared by God, his Maker. He would not be a spiritual automaton, forced to live in any particular way. He would be a "free" creature, able to choose and reject, thus, able to love and hate.

Indeed, it is the freedom of man that accounts for many of humanity's current maladies. We can bless, but we can also curse. We can make peace, but we can also make war. We can love, but we can also hate. Certainly, human freedom, in and of itself, does not guarantee love, nor does it guarantee evil; it only makes each choice possible. Nonetheless, it is true that man's freedom has caused the world a great deal of pain. It touches our lives and it touches God's heart. But He did not make a mistake in creating man. We ought to remember that God spoke with intention and He created with a purpose at the beginning of His new universe. We should ask, "What, then, was God's hope for mankind?"

I had an epiphany today. Not one outside the realm of orthodoxy I am sure. I realized, as I was shopping and walking among the crowds of people, most of us are oblivious to the Divine Presence. We walk, each in our own world, consumed, but not with God. Then I thought that more than anything, God wants our attention. He wants to know that we are thinking of Him, that our hearts often go to Him in love and fellowship, and that we acknowledge that there is nothing more precious to us than He. God's hope for creating was love, and no less than that. It is the loftiest experience of all free and living things—to be loved and adored and cherished.

"The Lord is near,"[137] longing after each one of our hearts. He desires our love and our attention more than anything, nevertheless, we find ourselves trapped in the vacuums of our own little worlds with no time to attend to our Maker, the Lover of souls. The saddest expression of that horrible neglect is found in Scripture: "In his pride the wicked does not seek him; in all his thoughts there is no room for God."[138] What a sad testimony, and God describes it with such pitiful sorrow: "There is no room for me."

We were made for God; this was His divine intent—to be known by His creation, in fellowship and in love. But for a relationship to grow and thrive, even a relationship between a person and God, there must be continuous and genuine attention; there must be a recognition of presence, love, and desire that is continually cultivated. Otherwise, one of the partners in that relationship will feel unappreciated, undesired, and unimportant. Human neglect of the Divine Presence does not paint a picture of our God as a pitiful and needy individual that wants our attention for validation and fulfillment, but rather, if we neglect God, we are only neglecting our place in the divine order of things.

Contrary to what we might think, God does not need us in the slightest; we need Him far more than we can comprehend.[139] Our spiritual neglect is like the problem of a worker bee, which upon reaching maturity, because of a defect is not able to follow its instinct. It cannot understand its job, and its place amongst the hive is lost. The bee is not good for much. It will not go out and perform its duties and thus fulfill its rightful place in life. It lives with no real purpose, lost in a larger community. And though it most certainly lives, it is not living to its fullest potential. It does not know its niche. God has given us a particular role to play in His creation, but like that poor little bee, we have lost our way.

Still, God wants our attention, and nothing will ever change that fact. The Old Testament is filled with types and shadows which point us to Christ and reveal to us the necessity of turning our attention toward God. One of the most beautiful examples can be found in the book of Numbers.

The people of Israel were grumbling against God and Moses, so God sent venomous snakes among the rebellious people. As a result, many were bitten and died. In spite of their previous behavior, the people cried out for mercy and asked Moses to intercede with God on their behalf. After Moses petitioned God for the people the Lord spoke these words, which if obeyed would grant life and healing to His people: "Make a snake and put it up on a pole; anyone who is bitten can look at it and live."[140] Symbolically, the snake represented the poison and sting of sin and death, while the pole represented the cross, on which Jesus of Nazareth died. Through that same cross, the power of sin and death was destroyed. The promise made by God so long ago pointed to the true healer, Jesus. He hung His Son on a cross and said that anyone who looked to Him would live, and be freed from their sin's sickness, just as they lived when they looked at the bronze snake. For this reason, Jesus said, "my Father's will is that everyone who looks to the Son and believes in him shall have eternal life...."[141]

Where we focus our attention is a direct function of the things in which we find value. To turn our attention toward God is to essentially say to Him, "You are valuable to me." God finds joy in our desire and attention. He does not need it, He craves it because our attention speaks words of love toward His throne: "You are valuable to me God—I need you, and I long to know you more."

A contemporary song that I often enjoy was written with words that convey a similar idea and a kindred desire that all renewed spirits share. "Oh Christ," the psalmist sings with a rigid passion, "be the center of our lives, be the place we fix our eyes...You're the center of the universe, everything was made in you. Breath of every living thing everyone was made for you."[142] The writer certainly had in mind the testimony of Paul: "For from him and through him and to him are all things."[143] Their words remind us of our place in the order of this world: we were made for God.

Sin has its beginnings in a rebellion to the divine order. So that is what sin is, and what it will always be: a refusal to conform to the order of God. Society is the perfect picture, because where we find order we find life, beauty and goodness, yet where we find rebellion there is death, destruction and evil. Order is important to the welfare of civilization, and it is vital to the progress of our spiritual lives. The most beautiful purpose of God's divine intent was to make free creatures with the capacity to love. Those who discovered their niche in the divine purpose are those who honored the order of creation and found beauty in the divine intent. But for every Abel there is a Cain, for every David, there is a Saul, and for every Peter, there is a Judas. There are those who look to God for their purpose and find their place in the order of God's creation, and conversely, there are others who do not want God and despise the divine intent.

Nevertheless, God, in love and sovereignty that we cannot fathom, placed us each perfectly in time and space. He further graced us each with equal and fair opportunity to respond to His loving presence: to conform to the beauty of the divine order. Truly, "he determined the times set for us and the exact places we should live...." But if we do not attend to His presence and love, what type of life remains available for us to live? What other purpose worth fulfilling can we ever hope to find? We exist for Him and only in Him can we find life everlasting. His Son entered our world, "that [we] may have life, and have it to the full."[144]—that we might discover our purpose, and find our place in the grand scheme of things.

It is true that this world is fallen. Its history and its people attest to that fact. And God knew how His creation would turn out. A sovereign God could know no less. He knew that many would turn their faces from the intent of creation, and as a result, bring chaos and sadness to this universe. We might ask, though, in light of that fact, "If God knew the result of His actions, why then did He create?" C.S. Lewis provides the curious seeker with a simple and satisfying answer: "Of course God knew what would happen if [humans] used their freedom the wrong way: apparently He thought it was worth the risk."[145] Again, the four words found at the beginning of our story serve as a glorious reminder: "In the beginning God—" This same God is still free, and He still in control. God's hope has never changed; He wants us for Himself.

We look out into space and call the amount of the stars in the sky innumerable, but to God they are not. He knows their number, and He calls them each by name. Take a look outside and in an instant try to count to the leaves on five trees. You cannot do it, but God can. Try to look in the mirror and count the hairs on your head. You cannot do it, but God can. What might be a monumental problem to the universe is only a small chip off the tiniest pebble to the Creator of Heaven and Earth.

We ought to realize that "the world is moving toward a pre-determined end, and God Almighty, who is standing in the shadows, is seeing it go, watching it and guiding it."[146] Purpose exists, and we find ours in God. This is why must heed the words of Isaiah and "Seek the LORD while he may be found; call on him while he is near."[147] Because He longs to be close to us; He ordered creation to that end, and He has made enjoying His presence man's highest and most glorious purpose.

In order to love God, our spiritual and moral freedom was an unavoidable necessity. Providence knew this, and He established this creation with that very fact in mind. As Andrew Murray said, "This is the nobility of man, that he has a will that can cooperate with God in understanding and approving and accepting what He offers to do."[148] That He can submit to the order that God has established, experiencing the wonders of his existence in the fullness of all God's divine intention. That He can love, and so fulfill His purpose, fitting in finely and splendidly into the sovereign order of creation.

ALL THINGS EXIST FOR HIM

    As a finale to His creative work, our heavenly Father created man. Every other creature in existence was privileged to witness the moment that God formed the crown of His creation. If the stars had eyes, they too would have witnessed the day that man was made, and rejoiced. The Lord counted the cost of creation, the evil that would have to be endured for the hope of love, and in sovereignty that only He possesses, decided that our hearts were worth the risk.

    The King eternal, immortal, invisible stands before us in majesty and brilliant love, revealing Himself through the image of His Son. To be sure, Jesus Christ is the radiance of God's glory and the dawning light that brightens our worlds. He is the morning star that rests in the sky as a divine signet to the earth that a new day has come. In love, He waits for our attention to shift; He waits for our vision to move toward the heavens, to see His glory appear on the horizon.

    The eyes of our hearts fixed and focused on Christ is what God wants more than anything else in the universe. He created this world with order and intent. Man was not made for the universe, but the universe was made for man, and man was made for God.[149] Therefore, all things exist for Him.

> "For this is what the LORD says—he who created the heavens, he is God; he who fashioned and made the earth, he founded it; he did not create it to be empty, but formed it to be inhabited—he says: 'I am the LORD, and there is no other. I have not spoken in secret, from somewhere in a land of darkness; I have not said to Jacob's descendants, 'Seek me in vain.' I, the LORD, speak the truth; I declare what is right. Gather together and come; assemble, you fugitives from the nations. Ignorant are those who carry about idols of wood, who pray to gods that cannot save. Declare what is to be, present it—let them take counsel together…there is no God apart from me, a righteous God and a Savior; there is none but me. Turn to me and be saved, all you ends of the earth; for I am God, and there is no other.'" Isaiah 45:18-22

-10-
I WAS NOT AWARE

Thoughts on the Gaze of God and the Divine Presence

"'Am I only a God nearby,' declares the LORD, 'and not a God far away? Can anyone hide in secret places so that I cannot see him?' declares the LORD. 'Do not I fill heaven and earth?'"
Jeremiah 23:23-24

How often do we stop to appreciate the simplicity of life? By that, I mean really the fact that we are *alive*. The fact that we can enjoy a sunrise and a sunset, that we can enjoy new birth, and reminisce about wonderful times with a loved one who has passed away should fill our hearts with some wonderful feelings about the joys and the blessing of life.

Each day the simplicity of life surrounds us, begging us to interact with it. At dawn and dusk, the sun paints the sky on the horizon with reds and golds and blues that warm our hearts, hoping that we would look up and smile at the beauty it prepares for us. The hummingbird hovers above as if held in midair by some magical force, waiting for us to recognize the mastery of its flight and be held in awe. Moreover, how often does that man in the moon look down from his home in the heavens to smile at us, waiting for us to respond in kind?

There is life all around us, but we are not aware of it. We lose ourselves in the activity of our shallow lives and wonder why we are so unhappy.

Love is invisible to our eyes, but tangible to our hearts. Life and Love reach out to us, but we refuse to take their hand. They offer themselves to us as wonderful gifts, but we squander their presence by looking away to what we think to be important. In the latter part of our lives, when true life and true love have almost escaped us, we look to them then, reaching with our hearts to grab them, wondering what could have been, asking ourselves why we never pursued them in our younger years.

Then we remember that we were blind at the time, and as beautiful as they may have been, in our hearts, we were not interested; we had more important desires. We had greater pursuits ahead of us—none that we reached of course—and none that could satisfy the hunger of our hearts. These were long-forgotten pursuits, faded pictures, things that did not, or that could not, follow us into our futures. Our lives moved forward and our trivial pursuits, are remembered if only as a dream. Long ago, those unfaithful friends abandoned us and left us all alone—lifeless, loveless, and ultimately incomplete.

There is hope for us yet. The One we need is near, in patience and love we cannot comprehend. He speaks when we take the time to attend to His presence: "I have loved you with an everlasting love; I have drawn you with loving-kindness."[150] It is certainly not God who ever abandoned us. He stands before us with arms open wide, hoping we will give Him the opportunity to bless us with the glories of His presence.

God is everywhere present. There is no portion of the universe that can resist the presence of His love or the penetration of His sight. No height can escape Him and no depth can hide from Him. No darkness can obscure His gaze, and all is consumed by His immanent presence. He knows us completely and perfectly, more thoroughly than we can ever hope to know ourselves. His all-seeing eye watches over us, while His presence looms near us; His voice speaks to us, while His love longs to know us. He says, "My sheep know my voice," but today we have forgotten the Shepherd.[151] We have turned away from His voice and neglected His loving call, failing to recognize that He is drawing us towards His heart with loving kindness. He desires us with passion we cannot comprehend, and He gazes at our hearts with a love that knows no degree. Each of us, He loves the same. Sadly, we have forgotten, "The Lord is near."

Nicholas of Cusa, the late Christian mystic, compares the all-seeing and all-loving gaze of our Creator to a picture, an icon of sorts.[152] Now if we imagine this vision of a man whose eyes, by the skill of the artist's hands, appear to be omnivoyant and watchful, and then see ourselves standing in a large room with that icon, if we were to set our gaze at the image, it would appear to be staring directly at us. It would seem as if the icon were able to follow wherever we cared to go.

But the watchful gaze of the image is not only toward the individual. If in our imaginations we were to place a thousand other strangers in that same room with us, the gaze of the icon would fix itself on each person, while never removing itself from even one.

To this thinker, it was a picture of God as His loving-gaze focused on the hearts of mankind. It was personal to the one, and yet also to the many.

> For, if I move, its glance seemeth to move because it quitteth me not; if, while I am moving, another look on the face while standing still, its glance in like manner, quitteth not him, but standeth still as he doth.[153]

Undeniably, no one in all creation is hidden from His sight. To this teacher of the contemplative spiritual life, the gaze of God was the watchful presence of the Divine Mystery. It was God looking upon us with longing and loving eyes, eyes that delight in our hearts, following us like that icon, wherever we dared go.

Certainly, because He is God, He must automatically know us all, see us all, and hear us all. His omniscience and His omnipresence assure the fact of His knowledge of us and His nearness to us. But knowing, seeing, and hearing does not automatically infer loving. We know, see, and hear those around us, but we do not necessarily love them.

As to alleviate any possible confusion, however, Jesus Christ tells us without reservation that "God so loved *the world.*"[154] By "the world" we must take His eternal words to mean something universal. His knowledge is unlimited, His presence undeterred, and His hearing unobstructed, yet He loves us still. While seeing all of our faults, being present during all of our sins, and hearing all of our evil words, He still loves in the midst of sin. Further, the Scriptures confirm that fact when in the book of Romans the Apostle Paul tells us the following: "God demonstrates his own love for us in this: While we were still sinners, Christ died for *us.*"[155] By "us," he of course means *the world*.

At the dawn of time, God painted for us a picture of His love. Let our minds float to the heavens and our hearts imagine what we have never seen with our eyes—a limitless universe where God is everywhere present, where planets and stars outnumber the grains of sand on a beach, and then let the Spirit of God return our thoughts to the Earth. He shows us our unique planet in a universe that cannot be measured, and He assures us that His gaze attends to what would seem to be an insignificant and small world. Yet, He formed it, and He alone loves it with an endless and tenacious love.

Then we think of the stars and the planets again, and we replace them with *the world*. We realize from this, of course, that God loves each of us uniquely, as much as He loves us all. Though we each might be one, tiny and insignificant, like the Earth among the heavens, He formed us, He sees us, and He loves us as no one else can.

Sadly, we think of Him as so far from us when in reality, He is closer than we can even perceive, always forgetting that great phrase "the heavens, even the highest heavens, cannot contain him."[156] We must remember, though, "He is there as He is here and everywhere, not confined to tree or stone, but free in the universe, near to everything, next to everyone, and through Jesus Christ immediately accessible to every loving heart."[157] But we ignore the gift of life, and tell ourselves that we are human. We ignore the blessedness of love, and tell ourselves that we are alive. We ignore God, and tell ourselves that we are satisfied—that we have everything we need. Then we go about our lives, filling it with hollow pursuits and empty dreams when a world of possibilities is available to each one of us.

We hide our inward longing and go about the business of living. We place a veil over our hearts and hope the world cannot see our pain. Adam and Eve hid from Him in the Garden, but they hid themselves to no avail. He saw them before He even called out searching, and He sees us before we even think to hide ourselves from His presence. This is the truth that inspired King David's worship. "O LORD," he said, "you have searched me and you know me. You know when I sit and when I rise; you perceive my thoughts from afar. You perceive my going out and my lying down; you are familiar with all my ways."[158]

He knows that we are hungry and He longs to satisfy our souls. Of course, if we took the time to discover what a beautiful blessing His divine affection is, sanity and wisdom might set in, and we might realize that God alone is what our hearts desire.

For our lives to change, we must know that God sees us and loves us, and also, that He longs to be near. When God descended upon Mount Sinai in the presence of Israel, He was next to each individual, as near to them as He was to the top of Sinai where His glory manifested for all to see. But God would not allow them to touch the mountain where His glory dwelt.[159] They could not experience the manifestation of His presence. Moses, however, was able to approach in faith only because God allowed.

We need not remain at the foot of the mountain, dissatisfied and disconnected from God, as many of the Israelites were in the days of Moses. If we have met His condition of faith, hope and love, God assures us that we can approach Him safely, in the hopes of a genuine spiritual experience with His manifest presence. The words of James encourage us to shun the fear, "draw near to God," he says to those who hope in Christ Jesus, "with a sincere heart in full assurance of faith, having our hearts sprinkled to cleanse us from a guilty conscience and having our bodies washed with pure water."[160]

He was present to the entire nation of Israel, next to every human soul, but only one heart was able to approach Him freely to taste the glory of His presence. Truly, God is holy; He is completely separate and opposed to sin. This is why Israel could not touch Mount Sinai when His presence descended.

We see this fact made clear to us throughout Scripture, but with loving kindness, in purifying grace, He allows us to draw near if we approach with a repentant heart, as did all who preceded us in true worship of our Maker and Lord.[161]

God is always the initiator of our genuine spiritual pursuits. If we are truly seeking after a relationship with God, it is only because God first sought after us. He is the beginning and the end of our spiritual strivings. He is the end of desire, but He too is its initiator. It is no wonder we are hungry—God has made us so.

When we realize that He is close and ready to satisfy, we are drawn to Him, and He to us. Repentant love can allow the unrighteous to draw near to the foot of the mountain, toward the heights of Jehovah, and thus, to experience the goodness of the divine Love.

He is attentive to our hearts and watches over our lives with careful Providence. At the dawn of creation, God made only one person, as all of His works enjoyed this creative act. He could have made millions, billions, or even trillions in less time than it took to make even the one. He did plan for more to come, of course, but in the beginning He formed a singular man, with a singular heart.

Among millions of Hebrews, we only have record of God presenting Himself to Moses in the form of a burning bush. He later called that same Moses to the top of Mount Sinai alone. He is far more personal than we often perceive Him to be. His glory certainly rests, as it did in the days of Moses, on a high peak above the earth. In majesty and glory, He is high above the universe. Yet, the fact that His glory rests above us at heights we cannot comprehend does not mean He prefers to be apart from us. On the contrary, God wants us as close to Him as we desire to be. He wants to gather us to Himself as His most treasured possession.

Indeed, He sits on His throne above the heavens. Beyond the edges of our universe, He stands in glory, power and presence behind a brilliant light our eyes cannot penetrate. Yet in unmistakable love, His omnivoyant gaze watches us each one by one, enjoying every moment that we choose to spend with Him, rejoicing when one of His created children is drawn by the power of His love. Undoubtedly, our attention is what He wants more than anything.

Just as the sun in the morning rises to warm the face of the earth, and shines brightly on the faces of those creatures that look toward it for warmth, so too, the Creator's glory falls down on us. His passion for us shines brightly on the face of each person that looks toward Him for light, revelation, and love, with a spiritual radiance that cannot be matched. But we must also remember that this same passion falls, like the icon of Nicholas of Cusa, on "*all things* and *each thing* at one and the same time."

The Scriptures speak to the fact that God's presence is near us all. With eternal words it declares this great reality, and it reminds us of the reason for our existence.

> From one man he made every nation of men, that they should inhabit the whole earth; and he determined the times set for them and the exact places where they should live. God did this so that men would seek him and perhaps reach out for him and find him, though he is not far from each one of us.[162]

Unfortunately, like Adam and Eve, when we realize that we are sinful, we hide ourselves from the God whom the earth cannot even contain. But where can we go from His presence?[163] When we realize we cannot escape the infinite presence of God, our lives will be different. Instead of running from that Great Presence, perhaps we will confess our evil ways and allow Him to overtake our hearts. His infinite presence condescends to inhabit the hearts of His children who have cried out for satisfaction and a clean heart. His glory, love, and Spirit will rest within and permeate every part of our existence. We will not see Him with our eyes, but with hearts of faith we will perceive the nearness of His love within, as His Spirit faithfully reminds us that we are in Him, and that He, forever, is in us.[164]

We can look at the world today and come to the right conclusion that most of us ignore the presence of God, and this is why the world is the way it is. He has always been close enough for us to enjoy His love, yet in our hearts, we do not care to be near.

Maybe one day when the time is right, when the dawn is near, and when the darkness has released its hold of us, perhaps the light of day will awaken us from our sleep, and like Jacob we will ponder in silence and reverence that great testimony of revelation: "Surely the LORD is in this place, and I was not aware...."[165]

> "Yet I am always with you; you hold me by my right hand. You guide me with your counsel, and afterward you will take me into glory. Whom have I in heaven but you? And earth has nothing I desire besides you. My flesh and my heart may fail, but God is the strength of my heart and my portion forever. Those who are far from you will perish; you destroy all who are unfaithful to you. But as for me, it is good to be near God." Psalm 73:23-28a

YOUR VOICE IS SWEET

Thoughts on Chaos, Order, and the Blessed Word of the Lord

"You came near and stood at the foot of the mountain while it blazed with fire to the very heavens, with black clouds and deep darkness. Then the LORD spoke to you out of the fire. You heard the sound of words but saw no form; there was only a voice...Ask now about the former days, long before your time, from the day God created man on the earth; ask from one end of the heavens to the other. Has anything so great as this ever happened, or has anything like it ever been heard of? Has any other people heard the voice of God speaking out of fire, as you have, and lived?"
Deut 4:11-12, 32-33

At certain moments in the account of Scripture, the terror connected to seeing God's presence and standing before Him is similar to that felt when hearing His voice. God's holiness is terrifying because it makes humans aware of their sin, and that awareness reminds us that, because we are impure, we cannot remain in His presence without incurring His wrath. It is not surprising that after hearing the song of the seraphs who worshipped in the majesty of God, Isaiah was filled with fear. After being reminded of the glorious truth of God by their harmony, "Holy, holy, holy is the LORD Almighty…," Isaiah responded in terror saying, "I am ruined! For I am a man of unclean lips…my eyes have seen the King, the LORD Almighty."[166]

In holiness, God's presence and voice are one in the same. A multitude of verses utter the same sentiment: "The voice of the LORD is powerful…."[167] It shakes the foundations of the heavens and the earth, so the dread that it often produces in creatures such as us is understandable to say the least.

A sun of comfort rises in our hearts when we read His written Word. We realize that only in hearing His voice is new life birthed within us. At the beginning of all things "He spoke and it came to be…," and we are encouraged continually to hearken to His Word.

God wants us to hear Him, and He alone will enable us to stand in His presence as He speaks. He cleansed Isaiah and took away the guilt of his sin; He is willing to do the same for us so that we can listen patiently to His voice as well.

How necessary is it for us to hear the divine voice? Jesus says, "I tell you the truth, a time is coming and has now come when the dead will hear the voice of the Son of God and those who hear will live."[168] The implication here was that those who were listening to His words then, and many today, were dead in their spirits, but those who listened to His direction would be made alive for the first time, just as those who looked to the bronze snake would live if they listened and obeyed His Word.

If we want to live as we never have before, we will attend to the voice of the Master as He speaks life-giving words into our broken and empty worlds, just as He did at the beginning of creation and as He did through Jesus Christ. The physical world cannot satisfy our internal hunger, and it cannot give us the life we so desperately need. We need to hear from Heaven because "man does not live on bread alone but on every word that comes from the mouth of the LORD."[169]

With that said, we should look at the situation realistically, in light of the spiritual temperament of the world. Probably one of the most difficult parts of our faith to accept is the proposition that a perfect and glorious eternal Being, if He did exist, would actually *speak* to simple and small human beings. Certainly, He has more important things to attend to.

To utter the words, "God speaks to me," in a public rather than private setting is to relinquish much of our personal credibility. We run the risk of alienating ourselves from those around us if we admit to this glorious truth unashamedly. The concept is strange to some and for many unbelievable, but those who have a difficulty grasping this spiritual truth are those who do not understand the position of mankind in the order of God's creation and our rightful place in His heart. If they knew how much God loved us they might be more willing to except the fact that divine communication is not only possible, but in a sense, it is very normal. I certainly do not mean to imply that God's voice speaking is *common* in the sense that it is not special or holy, but by *common* I mean it is the proper, spiritual result of a thriving and growing relationship with our Eternal Father.

Even in our personal human relationships, we become more closely acquainted with the voice of those we love the more time we spend in their presence communicating with them. Therein, we find the answer to our query. *God speaks to us, because He loves us.*

Assuredly, God has already spoken, but He still speaks

today. He has never stopped speaking to the hearts and the souls of His beloved people. They would not have survived had His voice stopped speaking. What a terrible day that would have been. We cannot imagine the sadness that would come to our world if God kept silent. If He shut His mouth, our world would fall into chaos in a matter of seconds. There would be no hope left for anyone. Truly, He sustains all things by His powerful Word,[170] and this is why we need Him to continue speaking to our hearts.

At the end of the matter, the world's opinion should not be important to us at all. Let them be considered "normal" while we commune with the Ancient of Days and listen to His peaceful, comforting and powerful words—the eternal Word that long ago brought light into darkness, and that today brings hope into our lives.

Personal salvation for the Christian not only relates to a future promise, but a present hope. God is calling us to Himself, and while we still take in this natural air as life to our bodies, we can begin to take into our spirits the air of His presence and voice, which will quicken our hearts as it quickened the world of old. His voice of love speaks to our hearts, and if we would heed His Word and follow its direction, our lives would definitely be changed for the better. For this reason, the Scripture reminds us, "the eyes of the Lord are on the righteous, and his ears are attentive to their prayer."[171] Our Master and Maker not only see us, but He listens intently to our voices, hoping we would take the time to speak to Him, since He is always trying to speak to us.

The words of Scripture give us an indication as to the intimacy and the holiness that our relationship reflects. Generally speaking, God hears everyone and sees everyone, but of the righteous, the repentant, the faithful remnant, it says His eyes are *on* us and His ears *attend* to our cries. If we would love enough to return the favor and make our ears and hearts attentive to His Word, then we would experience an indescribably brilliant quality of internal and vibrant, spiritual life.

The words of Jesus, as He prayed to the Father, remind us how important God's Word is to our lives:

> I am coming to you now, but I say these things while I am still in the world, so that they may have the full measure of my joy within them. I have given them your word and the world has hated them, for they are not of the world any more than I am of the world. My prayer is not that you take them out of the world but that you protect them from the evil one. They are not of the world, even as I am not of it. Sanctify them by the truth; your word is truth.[172]

When He speaks, His words shake us at our very foundations just as they shake the earth; the consuming fire of His Word brings light into darkness. It changes us from the inside out, burning off all the dross and imperfection of the corrupted life by which we were once enslaved and bound. Yet, our Lord's words also reveal to us the hatred the world shows toward those who listen to His voice. "I have given them your word and the world has hated them, for they are not of the world any more than I am of the world." In one regard, Christians are hated throughout the world because God speaks to them. His Word is hidden within their hearts, and His voice is among them. This makes them holy, and holiness, the world hates.

To be sure, God's mode of communication is, for the most part, distinctively different from our own; His voice speaks to our hearts and our spirits. We have ears to hear and eyes to see the external, material world, but God's voice is immaterial. He is Spirit, and only through our spirits does divine fellowship occur. We read His written Word and His voice speaks to our hearts. Foreigners and aliens we are, our spiritual language is distinctly different. There are no lessons or schools by which we can learn this new dialect. This mystical speech is taught by the Father of our hearts as we spend time in His presence, attending to His written Word. Until we respond to His voice, we will find ourselves incurably illiterate. It will take desire and passion, but if we find that hunger for God's voice within, our lesson will certainly begin.

To understand the importance of His voice and Word in our lives, let us refer back to the beginning of Creation. What was it that brought light into darkness and infused divine order into a chaotic and formless world? Was it not the voice of the Almighty, the One who "[speaks] things that are not as though they were"?[173]

He not only brought radiant, inextinguishable light into a dark universe, but He brought order to creation through the power of His voice. This same order is what we may look forward to in faith, just as Abram looked forward to the fulfillment of God's promises in his life. It is up to us whether or not we, like the creation, will obey His voice and witness a change in our worlds, just as the patriarch Abram did when he obeyed God's Word and trusted in His promise. The author of Genesis tells us the story of creation, and with three short sentences, He reveals the power that can change our lives.

> In the beginning God created the heavens and the earth. Now the earth was formless and empty, darkness was over the surface of the deep, and the Spirit of God was hovering over the waters. And God said, 'Let there be light,' and there was light.[174]

Indeed He was there, with divine patience we cannot understand, waiting eagerly to bring order to the world that He formed for by an act of His will, and that for His own good pleasure.[175] He was there, and He is here now. Before each successive act of creation He spoke, and the universe obeyed His voice. The beautiful creation we now enjoy, though marred by sin because of man's folly, is the unique result of His voice speaking and establishing beauty and divine order.

> By the word of the LORD were the heavens made, their starry host by the breath of his mouth. He gathers the waters of the sea into jars; he puts the deep into storehouses. Let all the earth fear

the LORD; let all the people of the world revere him. For he spoke, and it came to be; he commanded, and it stood firm.[176]

There are many troubling problems with our world today, but God's sovereign hand is still working to fulfill His purposes, and although this world has much evil in it, there is still much beauty to enjoy.

His voice is the most important sound we will ever hear. Sadly, so many of us today are like those of whom Jesus spoke when He said, "Though seeing, they do not see; though hearing, they do not hear or understand...For this people's heart has become calloused..."[177]

We must be sure not to follow the example of Adam and Eve who hid when they heard the presence of God in the Garden of Eden, because they were aware of their nakedness and their sin. Nor should we be as those in the days of Moses who, when God spoke, shuddered in fear and dread and begged not to hear His voice again:

> When you heard the voice out of the darkness, while the mountain was ablaze with fire, all the leading men of your tribes and your elders came to me. And you said, 'The LORD our God has shown us his glory and his majesty, and we have heard his voice from the fire. Today we have seen that a man can live even if God speaks with him. But now, why should we die? This great fire will consume us, and we will die if we hear the voice of the LORD our God any longer.'[178]

In fear of judgment, they cowered at the sound of His holy voice, as that holiness convicted them of their sin, asking Moses to stand in the gap for them. But the Scripture tells us that now, through faith, we can stand in the presence of our holy God and not withdraw in fear. We can stand boldly in His glory and listen to the Divine Voice speaking to us from His throne in the heavens, high above and far away in majesty and infinity, yet nearer to our hearts than we can ever know.

Those who hid from His voice did not realize what the trial

of Shadrach, Meshach, and Abednego taught: If we stand in the fire with the Son of Man beside us, we will not be destroyed; we will glow with the glory of Heaven, as those faithful and holy Hebrews did next to their Savior and Protector. They stood in a fire that consumed all who came near, but were themselves not scorched by the flames.[179]

God also wants us to come near to the fire of His presence: to attend to the glory of His voice. If we are brave enough to approach, all that is not of Heaven will be burned away as the ties that bound the young Hebrews were, and only what He has done in our hearts will remain.[180] The deeper into His fiery presence we press through increasing holiness, the more clear His magnificent voice becomes in our hearts.

As long as we have opportunity, we must listen to that voice and hearken to its message. We are reminded by the mysterious author of the book of Hebrews, "God again set a certain day, calling it Today...."[181] He further implores us to obey His command He delivered so long ago:

> See to it, brothers, that none of you has a sinful, unbelieving heart that turns away from the living God. But encourage one another daily, as long as it is called Today, so that none of you may be hardened by sin's deceitfulness. We have come to share in Christ if we hold firmly till the end the confidence we had at first. As has just been said: 'Today, if you hear his voice, do not harden your hearts....'[182]

If we would open our hearts to listen and respond in faith to His Word, a new creation will begin within us. Order will appear in a life that seemed to be destined for chaos, and we will inevitably enjoy the beauty of the Divine Voice speaking words of love into our hearts.

"Here I am!" He says. "I stand at the door and knock. If anyone hears my voice and opens the door, I will come in and eat with him, and he with me."[183] Like the gentleman that He is, He will enter only at our request. It does no good in our lives if we merely hear God speak to us, but do nothing in response. If we are willing to listen, He will speak to us out of the fire of His presence and the darkness of His mystery, bringing order and purpose into our lives. He will expel the chaos and reveal His Providence.

Leading us to green pastures and beside quiet waters as a shepherd leads his sheep, He will call us each by name and we will follow because we finally know His voice.[184] Unlike those who dwelt in the wilderness with Moses, we will not turn away in fear and ask Him not to speak to us. When we hear His voice from out of the fire, our plea will be like that of the longing lover in the Song of Solomon, "let me hear your voice, for your voice is sweet."[185]

> "See to it that you do not refuse him who speaks. If they did not escape when they refused him who warned them on earth, how much less will we, if we turn away from him who warns us from heaven? At that time his voice shook the earth…since we are receiving a kingdom that cannot be shaken, let us be thankful, and so worship God acceptably with reverence and awe, for our 'God is a consuming fire.'" Hebrews 12:25-29

-12-

BECAUSE I AM HOLY

THOUGHTS ON THE FRAILTY OF MAN, THE GRACE OF GOD, AND THE SOURCE OF OUR PERFECTION

"'Even now,' declares the LORD, 'return to me with all your heart, with fasting and weeping and mourning.' Rend your heart and not your garments. Return to the LORD your God, for he is gracious and compassionate, slow to anger and abounding in love…."
Joel 2:12-13

Although we say that God loves us unconditionally, we cannot therefore presume, because of that marvelous truth, that He is always pleased with who we are and with the ways in which we choose to live. In the same way, a mother can love us unconditionally, but still not be satisfied with how we have chosen to live our lives. Her love compels her to still desire our attention, fellowship, and affection, but we cannot conclude that she is content if we live our lives in a way that does not represent the values she expects us to hold. We will discover a similar displeasure if we take the time to figure out who God truly is, and the lifestyle He expects of us as His children.

Most people today spend more time following their favorite sitcom than they do trying to figure out who God really is. Our spiritual exercises are minute at best, and they seem to indicate a strong lack of interest. We say we want to know more about the Divine Mystery, but the world has so many philosophies and so many teachers that it is hard to pick just one, while excluding all the others. Our task would be much easier, however, if we did not always settle for such a low view of God. None of that matters anyway, however, because our lives indicate the truth. The true knowledge of God, which comes through prayer, patience, effort, study, and revelation, is not very important to most of us. It requires far too much effort.

With things the way they are, we accept a very superficial view of God and His love; then, we set our hearts on "cruise control," as if our knowledge is taking us to a grand new world and we are taking in the air and scenery of this empty life on the way.

The Scripture tells us our blessing is found a different way, when it reminds us that "anyone who comes to [God] must believe that he exists and that he rewards those who *earnestly* seek him."[186] Diligence today in regard to spiritual matters is a difficult thing to find, and diligence that is not misplaced is even rarer. Spiritual truth takes time and effort to learn, and if we forsake the work, our treasure will be small. Thankfully, a wealth of value and richness is uncovered as we seek after the knowledge of God in humility and love and desire.

Certainly, "God so loved the world," but that unconditional love does not remove His desire that the hearts of those who return to Him be cleansed. He wants them to seek after Him in diligence with an earnest heart if they want to be rewarded with true, spiritual blessing. If we truly knew Him in righteousness, holiness, and majesty we would understand why. God loves us as we are, but He is not content to keep us as we are. God is looking to make better people out of us. *He* cannot change, and He does not need to change, since He is perfect. We, however, should embrace the fact that *we* can change. God wants to enhance our character: He wants to make us holy people.

Other religions that attempt to point men to God make a horrendous error; they give us the impression that through our efforts and actions we can please God and satisfy any requirement He sets before us. But God is not impressed or pleased with what we try to do to earn His favor—He is appalled. The Scripture is true, "All of us have become like one who is unclean, and all our righteous acts are like filthy rags."[187] This means our efforts to prove ourselves worthy of His favor are insignificant to say the least.

Too often, the world gives its children the impression that God is satisfied and will always be satisfied with who we are. Yet, not even the most loving mother would deceive her child with the notion that any way of living is healthy and productive. Although she would love that child with all of her heart, that same love would compel her to warn them if their chosen lifestyle were a danger. Because of her love, the mother cannot be silent. Neither can our God of love be quiet when His children's souls are at risk.

"O wretched man that I am!"[188] is the testimony of a person in touch with the frailty of their human spirit, and certainly God loves us, draws us, and calls us to Himself as we are; however, He wants, needs, and enables us to change for the better. God is holy; He is set apart from sin and sinners. The ominous words of the prophet Habakkuk compound the issue for us: "Your eyes are too pure to look on evil; you cannot tolerate wrong."[189]

The fool says to himself, "God has forgotten; he covers His face and never sees."[190] But the wise man speaks humble and contrite words, "God has not forgotten and I owe Him a great debt." If we cannot earn God's favor, and if He is not pleased with our vain attempts at self-righteousness, then how can He find any pleasure in us at all? If His eyes are, as Christians say, "too pure to look on evil," then how can God value men and women like us? This is a valid question, considering all the evil we see in the world today. Christians claim that God loves the world, but anyone looking at this world can see it is full of all kinds of evil.

God does love the world. He values its people, because He made them for Himself. While our sin causes God a tremendous amount of displeasure, He still, nonetheless, longs to be close to us. He does not want to be alienated from us forever, but He must do something about the filth of our hearts and lives, because He "cannot tolerate wrong."

When that man of the wild, John the Baptist, was immersing Jews in the wilderness, He was baptizing believers who wanted to repent of their sin—those who recognized that they needed to be cleansed by God. One day the perfect "lamb of God who takes away the sins of the world" went to meet John to be baptized. Jesus was not being baptized for repentance. John affirmed that fact when he said that Jesus should baptize him instead. He was perfectly holy, as the Son of God and our Great High Priest. He need not repent of anything. Yet, He came to be baptized to identify Himself with those sinners whom He had come to save.

God is set apart from sin and sinners in perfect holiness

that we cannot understand, but in equally mysterious love He is connected to us and wants to know us in fellowship and in love. Jesus' actions demonstrate both truths time and time again in Scripture. He made friends with those the world had scorned and despised. He made a habit of reaching out to people who knew they needed to be cleansed. Sin cannot enter His kingdom, but we are sinful people. It does create a lofty hurdle in our efforts to enjoy fellowship with God, but the Great Physician that He is, He is able to heal our sin's sickness.[191]

Now, when we are humble enough to agree with Him on the point of our being guilty of something that God knows about, He is ready, willing and very much able to do something about it. The way that God legitimately qualifies us for the perfection he requires is through something called "grace." They say that grace is a distinctly Christian concept. That it, in the way in which Christians know, cannot be found anywhere else. As such, the orthodox Christian doctrine on grace is, as some have said, one of Christianity's most distinctive teachings.

This idea of "unmerited favor," from the moment God revealed Himself to Adam, has been to the true and living faith, what iron and wood is to the structure and foundation of any building. Infused within the framework of that faith, "once and for all entrusted to the saints," is the idea that God is gracious toward us; the notion that God loves us so, and because of that, He graciously heals us from the sickness of our sin if we call out in faith and repentant love.

Grace is God's "Favor or kindness shown without regard to the worth or merit of the one who receives it and in spite of what that person deserves"[192] It is God's mercy and kindness expressed to those who could not earn it and to those who do not deserve it. Other traditions may talk about "grace," but its meaning in Christian theology and life is distinct. This divine grace is not only a theological teaching, a provision for our salvation and what is necessary for us to stand in the presence of our holy God who has a perfect standard, but it is also a true and living spiritual blessing. It is God telling us there is nothing we could do to lose His affection and nothing we could do to earn it. It is His devotion to imperfect creatures, to imperfect people. His arm reaching toward frail individuals who need help, hoping we will grab hold of His truth.

It is the "face" of God shining on the undeserving. For this reason, the prophet Moses said, "The LORD bless you and keep you; the LORD make his face shine upon you and be gracious to you; the LORD turn his face toward you and give you peace."[193] We need to see His face; there is no grace, nor peace to be found without it.

To be sure, no one can see God's true essence. No man can view it, no man can perceive it, and no man can endure it. Let us imagine that the power necessary to create the entire universe was harnessed in a single source of energy, and then let us imagine that the power contained by that source is infinite. Would it be safe to say that we, mere humans, the dust and clay that we are, would be destroyed in the presence of that awesome power? Absolutely, and this is the dilemma we face when we consider the problem of seeing God as He truly is. He condescends in love, so that we are not overwhelmed by the power of His infinite glory, but He is greater than we can imagine, and because of this, His true nature no man can see.

So in one respect we cannot see His face—that is, His nature. Yet, in the manner which is necessary for us to experience His love and to be deemed righteous in His sight, we are able to see His face—that is, His grace.

While God's standard is perfection, He is not one to hold creatures He loves so much to a standard so high without preparing a way for them to qualify for that glorious ideal.

The idea of divine perfection and holiness is an important standard to uphold, because it reminds us continually that we cannot win God's favor or pleasure on our own. Our lack of perfection disqualifies us from even entering into the competition. Then we are forced to ask ourselves the question: "How then can we draw near to God?"

In ourselves, we are all unqualified before Him. Because of that, His face is "set against us," and His awesome holiness causes great spiritual apprehension on our part. It was His holiness that prevented the Israelites from drawing near to the mountain where His glory dwelt, for they felt the fear that sinful people perceive when met with the revelation of a holy God. Remember Isaiah's response when He stood before the pinnacle of holiness, "I am ruined!" He said, "For I am a man of unclean lips...my eyes have seen the King, the LORD Almighty." This divine holiness causes us the same problem when we think about drawing near to God ourselves—a God whom we sin against time and time again. Standing before Him, we consider our iniquity, and if we are honest, we admit that we are guilty of some great errors. We lower our heads in shame, and realize we are not worthy of beholding His glorious face.

However, when we own up to our imperfection in humility, in faith, and in love, we are emboldened, enthralled and encouraged by His Holy Spirit, to gaze upon His shining face. The fool does not have the wherewithal to admit his wrongdoing, and he mocks the fact that he may be held accountable for his evil. But the proverb spoke about him long ago, "[God] mocks proud mockers but gives grace to the humble,"[194] reminding us that we should view ourselves in a proper light if we expect to partake in the grace of God.

For this reason, the living and enduring Word points to the source of our perfection, and while it reminds us that we were "dead in transgressions," it also declares that we have been made alive through Christ:

> Like the rest, we were by nature objects of wrath. But because of his great love for us, God, who is rich in mercy, made us alive with Christ even when we were dead in transgressions...And God raised us up with Christ and seated us with him in the heavenly

realms in Christ Jesus, in order that in the coming ages he might show the incomparable riches of his grace, expressed in his kindness to us in Christ Jesus…it is by grace you have been saved, through faith [in Christ Jesus]—and this [salvation is] not from yourselves, it is the gift of God—not by [your own] works, so that no one can boast.[195]

Jesus Christ is the elect One, the only One who is truly and perfectly qualified to stand before God in true righteousness and holiness. If we are found "in Him" by faith, we can stand before God's mighty throne, as long as we look to His perfect sacrifice to qualify us, and not to our won self-righteous effort. Christians are called to live special lives as a sign that they truly know Jesus Christ, and not as a method or a means to find salvation on their own.

It was sin that separated us from God's presence in the first place. We must constantly be reminded that sin cannot stand in the manifest presence of our holy God. For this reason, a flaming sword was placed in front of the perfect Garden in the beginning after man's original sin: the fire representing God's holiness, the sword the symbol of His wrath, and the garden the symbol of His perfect presence. If we ever forget about God's hatred of sin, we need only look back to the story in Genesis, and the majestic weapon He placed in the entryway to the Garden as an ominous reminder of His disdain for man's sin.

But God loves us so much, and because of His love we can look up to the heavens one day, when His Spirit has prepared our hearts for His Son, and before our eyes a shining face appears, glorious and new. Its benevolent light covers us with grace from Heaven, and saves us from the penalty of our sin.

Our spirits can safely move beyond that sword of fiery wrath that kept us, for so long, from enjoying the divine affection of His awesome and infinite love. A heart that is humble, who has been blessed with a vision of grace, can now gaze at the truth and the glories of God without fear of condemnation and without resenting His divine Creator. This heart now understands the purpose for which it exists. By faith, it can now look into His Divine Perfection, see His terrible holiness and righteous justice, while still feeling the warmth of His purifying love and the goodness of His tender mercies.

This new child, born out of the Spirit and not out of the flesh, never forgets the revelation of divine holiness, for it is that which encourages him to cleanse his heart continually. And he always remembers that he has been saved by grace, through faith in Jesus Christ alone. Nevertheless, he cannot forget the grand imperative penned by Peter, "just as he who called you is holy, so be holy in all you do; for it is written: 'Be holy, because I am holy.'"[196]

"Praise be to the God and Father of our Lord Jesus Christ, who has blessed us in the heavenly realms with every spiritual blessing in Christ. For he chose us in him before the creation of the world to be holy and blameless in his sight. In love he predestined us to be adopted as his sons through Jesus Christ, in accordance with his pleasure and will—to the praise of his glorious grace, which he has freely given us in the One he loves. In him we have redemption through his blood, the forgiveness of sins, in accordance with the riches of God's grace that he lavished on us with all wisdom and understanding." Ephesians 1:3-8

NO ONE WILL SEE THE LORD

Thoughts on True Worship, the Manifest Presence of God, and Perfecting Holiness

"At once I was in the Spirit, and there before me was a throne in heaven with someone sitting on it. And the one who sat there had the appearance of jasper and carnelian. A rainbow, resembling an emerald, encircled the throne. Surrounding the throne were twenty-four other thrones, and seated on them were twenty-four elders. They were dressed in white and had crowns of gold on their heads. From the throne came flashes of lightning, rumblings and peals of thunder…Whenever the living creatures give glory, honor and thanks to him who sits on the throne and who lives for ever and ever, the twenty-four elders fall down before him who sits on the throne, and worship him…." Revelation 4:2-5a, 9-10a

Across religions and within religions what we find referred to as "worship" of a divine being can range from a dry, apprehensive piety to an exciting, unabated enjoyment of spirituality. Generally, what we see on television or movies, or hear stories of in conversation fall into one of these two categories. Among Christian fellowships, we see these categorical distinctions as well.

The first category of worshippers emphasizes their religious experience as a rational construct which must be understood mentally and internally to have its premier enjoyment, while the other emphasizes their religious experience more in terms of a relationship rather than as a rational derivation of spiritual principles or truths. To the one, religion and its myriad of ideas and theology empower its spirituality, yet the other becomes impoverished when it is inhibited by the boundaries of religious thought and theological conceptions. The only reason there is such a sharp distinction between the two, is that these groups do not realize that they come from the same Father, and as such, neither can be called a family without the other.

Perhaps if they were to return to each other, their religious experience might find itself as having moved closer to the heart of the Father, and more reminiscent of those twenty-four elders who live in Heaven and worship Him "who lives for ever and ever." Our Grand Designer is divinely stunning, and no descriptions of His glory capture that splendor in its fullness. If there is one thing we learn from those attempts to verbalize His wonder, though, it is that God's splendor is far beyond all our common ideas of beauty, and He deserves true worship.

If, by His Spirit, we have truly glimpsed that divine charm and heavenly majesty, we will lay our hearts before Him and worship Him in love and adoration, as those who see Him now in Heaven do day and night.

We should always try to understand that truths exist as landmarks toward spiritual growth. We cannot rightly, and in increasing degree, worship a God we never come to know better, or come to see in the majesty of what He has revealed about His glory. Herein, we observe the necessity of understanding "religious" ideas.

Many of us do not truly know God in a way that would transform our shallow and vain exhibitions into worship that more closely resembles a true experience with the Creator of the heavens and the earth. Jesus said "a time is coming and has now come when the true worshipers will worship the Father in spirit and in truth, for they are the kind of worshipers the Father seeks."[197] Our worship should be spirited, but it should be directed and led by the Spirit of Heaven, in all righteousness, truth, and harmony. This is what God desires. We worship God in vain, if our so-called spiritual displays are motivated by external influences, as opposed to the Divine Presence that calls us to worship God in "truth" as well as "spirit."

In Scripture, I have no recollection of an encounter with God and the resulting human response that anyone would find in the least "hilarious" or "entertaining," in the way in which they are viewed today. Even after that blessed Pentecost when the Church was born as the Spirit descended on God's people, and caused them to speak in different tongues, many that were near the great commotion caused by God's manifestation were bewildered and amazed. Though some ignorant fools misunderstood what was happening and said that the early Christians were drunk, their lack of insight was corrected, and many people acknowledged that something special was indeed occurring. Peter had an opportunity to give a powerful defense of the gospel as a result of the outpour of the Spirit, and around three thousand people came to faith in Christ that day.

King David danced before the ark of the Lord "with all his might," and his Spirit-inspired psalms are often used by worshipers today to sing praises to the King of Glory. Yet, his leaping and dancing before the Lord, was typical of his heart of worship. He humiliated himself before God, not as a spectacle to other men, but as a king over God's people, who considered humility more valuable than dignified glory. His wife, who did not have in mind the things of God, was embarrassed at his spirited worship, but David did not bother himself with her concerns, for he had set his heart toward worshiping the true King, and no dignity was more valuable to him than that.[198]

But as examples of vibrant spirituality today, much of what we see is tickling and humorous, to say the least. This makes very little sense when we factor in the majesty of the God whom we serve. The only conclusion I can come to is that the spirituality of some today appears to be a tenuous emotional externality that results in very little inward change, and is very rarely produced by a genuine experience with the transcendent glory of God Most High. Exhibitionism, not worship, is what is motivating those counterfeit presentations of spiritual devotion. This is why the lives of many who appear to be "full of the Spirit" during their moments of worship reflect a lack of true devotion. There is no change, because there is no deep and holy meeting with God in the depths and the dark places of their hearts.

That being said, true worship is inspired and directed toward God, and as such, it must always have in mind the desire to bless Him and Him alone. It should reflect a desire to meet with God in love, to have Him visit us "in spirit and in truth," and to allow Him to make a deep and lasting change within us. The desire to please the external world should disappear continually, as it did for King David, and God's heart should be our most important concern.

We can never deny that whenever The Ancient of Days reveals His glory, His presence can be felt, and the Spirit certainly calls us to worship. But we must always have God in mind. We must always listen for His tenderness, His excitement, His jubilation, and His quietness. This is true worship, following the flow of God's Spirit, as He allows us to experience the manifestation of His presence. Our worship should be spirited, but it should also be tempered by the truth.

Indeed, if God has truly appeared among His people, their response should be indicative of that Presence, and it will be directed by His orderly Spirit. This can be witnessed as both an exuberant and ecstatic joyfulness or as an intimate and quietly reverent joy of heart; His glory, though, should not pass us unnoticed. When God shows up, all that is in us should be moved by His majesty, beauty, and love. I suspect that the true worshippers today are found somewhere in the happy medium between the "laughable" and the "dead." There, sincerity of heart is most likely found, and those are the worshipers God desires. Too often today, our genuine devotion is overshadowed by exhibitionism. We have lost sight of the glories of true worship, and might very well be able to worship God in "spirit," but the "truth" we need just as much.

In the scriptural account, truth is said to bring freedom; it only impoverishes those who would rather not have it. Emotion is not the enemy of spiritual experience or personal growth, but its expression must always be tempered by truth. If it is righteous, its inspiration will be of God. Truth is a gift from Heaven. There are some who are said to have hated the truth, but we should not imitate their example. We should long for truth, for when we know the truth, "the truth will set [us] free."[199]

A true worshipper not only knows the God whom he or she has been called to worship, but this person is growing each day in the knowledge of what that God expects, and in the experience and the joy of the bliss that accompanies His presence. To clarify, genuine religion is marked by a grand experience of God. The less recognizable that God is to us, the more base our worship of Him is. As a result, our spiritual fulfillment will certainly be lacking as well. Conversely, the more we come to know God, and adjust our lives according to that novel insight, the richer our enjoyment of Him becomes.

If we wanted to enjoy the beauty of the ocean in increasing degrees, we would have to make sure we were trained in how to swim, perhaps how to scuba, and maybe even how to sail. Otherwise, we would only be able to enjoy the shallows and even that only superficially, because of our fear to move out into the depths. We would always be apprehensive, and we would never be able to appreciate its finer beauties because we never took the time to learn what was necessary for us to enjoy it more fully. Our actions would indicate whether or not we were seafaring people, and our worship is indicative of how closely acquainted we are with God.

If we are to worship God rightly, and if we are to move out into the depths of beauty, we must know the glory of the One for whom we search. "A light has dawned" was the word of the prophet, and that light shines as our direction. If we turn our hearts toward it, we will walk in the light of life. We too will be moved to cast our crowns to the ground and give honor to the King eternal, immortal, invisible.

I have felt the manifest presence of God and seen its glory myself. I can say that the glow is unlike any natural light. It is probably the most supernatural experience I have ever had. It was holy like nothing I have ever known, and I long to taste it again. The glow of Heaven is near, it is ready to shine brightly within all our hearts, but there is effort required on our part, and there is a way we must travel to find it.

If we were traveling home from an unfamiliar place, we might have to face many different problems on our way. Even finding the correct highway to travel can be the most taxing thing about our journey, especially when there seems to be so many different ways we can go. Likewise, the same is true of our spiritual lives. There is a particular direction we should be traveling to find our spiritual satisfaction, and we definitely need to get some direction if we are ever going to find it. There are many people who claim to know a better way to get where our souls long to be, but we must careful we are traveling on the proper highway, because not all roads lead to the same place.

Many Christians speak to the quality of their unique experiences with the glory of God. One in particular described the moments of entry into God's presence, when He manifests His love among us, as such:

> In this inconceivable mountain of the supra-divine Where [the 'height of the divine Majesty transcending substance'] there is a precipitousness of which all spirits are sensible. Here the soul enters a secret namelessness, a marvelous alienation. It is the bottomless abyss no creature can sound—...the spirit perishes there, to become all-living in the wonders of the Godhead.[200]

But to travel that spiritual road and find that blessed experience that so many other human creatures have felt, there must be an increasing change within us. The Scriptures direct us back home to Glory. They tell us the name of that blessed Way.

> And a highway will be there; it will be called the Way of Holiness. The unclean will not journey on it; it will be for those who walk in that Way; wicked fools will not go about on it. No lion will be there, nor will any ferocious beast get up on it; they will not be found there. But only the redeemed will walk there, and the ransomed of the LORD will return. They will enter Zion with singing; everlasting joy will crown their heads. Gladness and joy will overtake them, and sorrow and sighing will flee away.[201]

The proper route to our spiritual home is the Way of Holiness. Now, in God we find a *perfect* holiness, meaning He is absolutely separate from anything impure. Yet, our task as His children is to allow Him to sanctify us continually by His Word and presence—that is, to allow Him to separate us from sin and the love of worldly things in increasing measure. As our hearts are purified more and more, our holiness enables us to perceive the manifest presence of God in increasing degree, as

He visits our hearts with precious visions of glory. Truly, as our love for Him increases, as our desire for His presence in our lives grows, and as our love for the guilty pleasures of the world diminishes, we will enjoy His presence more and more.

For this reason Paul said, "I urge you, brothers, in view of God's mercy, to offer your bodies as living sacrifices, holy and pleasing to God…"[202] He wants our entire person; not just our bodies, but our lives. He wants to consume us with the fire of His presence as He consumed the sacrifices offered in Ancient Israel. If we will offer ourselves to Him in holiness—a living sacrifice—He will not turn us away. He will consume our beings in unquenchable passion, and fill our hearts with joy.

Even our natural cleansing process gives insight into the necessity of continuous, spiritual purification as it relates to our connection to God. The norm of our society today is to at least observe a daily cleansing of our physical bodies. If we went even one day without observing our due diligence in this matter our lack would be clear and it would make it very difficult for others to enjoy being around us. The longer we neglected to clean ourselves, the more disgusting we would become. We live in a filthy world, and there are countless pollutants that must be removed from our bodies daily. And so it is with our spiritual selves. If we go a day or two without washing our hearts, its filth will be discernable. Each day, our minds and hearts must be purified from the things of the world. This is why the holy teacher, Paul, encouraged His brethren, "let us purify ourselves from everything that contaminates body and spirit."[203]

At the moment of conversion, we are washed by the Holy Spirit, and the stain of death, with all its penalties and worries, is removed. Still, each day we must be washed anew to grow ever closer to Him. This cleansing is called "perfecting holiness out of reverence for God."[204] We must remove the stains of the world in which we live that displease our Father, thus preparing ourselves to enter into His presence frequently throughout our lives. He is not a God who is disconnected from His people. He is very much connected to us by His Spirit, but perfecting holiness allows us to perceive God's continual presence in our lives.

It is true that the Scripture testifies "there is now no condemnation for those who are in Christ Jesus,"[205] but while we are not condemned for our sin any longer, we can still feel guilt when we live in a way that contradicts God's call to holiness. We would not have repentant hearts if we could not feel remorse and godly sorrow. But a heart that longs to be holy and separate from sin, that trusts in God for the power to resist temptation, and that trusts in Christ to continually remove its guilt, is one that will be able to press deeper and deeper into the throne room of the Master.

Sin causes a spiritual apprehension on our part as evidenced by Adam and Eve hiding from God after their sin in the garden. This is why over and over again He tells His people, "wash and make yourselves clean," so that the guilt of our sin will not cause us to retreat from His life-giving presence. So that God can take pleasure in our purity, and meet us often in love and experience.

The story of the temple sacrifices holds a wonderful illustration. Before entering into God's presence, the high priest had to purify himself, and if he entered into the presence of God in an unclean manner, he would die because of God's holy presence. We can stand before God in His holiness because of our trust in the sacrifice of Jesus, but to experience the surpassing joy of His manifest presence, we too must purify our hearts to prepare for entrance into the throne room of God. The "Way of Holiness" leads us to joy and peace, and a surpassing beauty of love we were created to enjoy.

As a blessed return for our love of holiness, the majestic and mysterious Maker of all that is will present a portion of Himself to us, as we are ushered into His presence by the Spirit. If our perspectives are true, we can realize that it is not simple emotion that we enjoy in this moment or even a common spiritual ecstasy; it is God Himself, the source of all goodness, whose nature is divine love. We feel what the mind can only describe as a mysterious and consuming fire, and within its heat, all that is not of God will melt away.

When God manifests Himself among His people:

> what was previously only possessed in insufficiency, only longed for, now comes upon the scene in living actuality, the experience of the transcendent in gracious intimate presence, the 'Lord's Visitation of His people.'[206]

The spirit of man was created to enjoy what the mind and the emotions could never fully understand, and that is why our experience of love can never be fully comprehended or explained with human language.

We try to conjure up images, fantasies and feelings in our minds that will help us to return to those moments, but when we do this, we are only returned to a fading image of love. Like words we write in a foggy mirror, the experience is clear for a time, and then, as the mist dissipates, what was clear becomes invisible again. It is still there, mind you, but we can only experience something reminiscent of the joy that is felt when those glorious moments have ended, and not a recurrence of the moment itself. The mind cannot take us where only the spirit was created to go. But when our hearts truly long for God alone, our imaginations cease, vain desires fade away, and only love and faith remain; then, the hope of glory can return in a grand manifestation. Then we would feel the glow of Heaven—the eternal love of God, burning with passion unmatched, like a consuming fire that melts away all of our imperfections, with a radiance that directs all of the soul's attention toward Heaven.

God is everywhere present, but the experience of His manifest presence is that which He graces us with when He reveals His glory. Hence the use of the word "manifest"—God must make Himself known to His people. We cannot penetrate the veil of divine mystery, but through His Spirit working within our hearts, God might make His presence a living reality before us, allowing us to enjoy His tender majesty. This is what Rudolf Otto spoke of in His classic work:

> The hours of His 'visitation' and His 'return' are rare and solemn occasions, different essentially not only from the 'profane' life of every day, but also from the calm confiding mood of the believer, whose trust is to live ever before the face of God. They are the topmost summits in the life of the spirit. They are not only rare occasions, they must needs be so for our sakes, for no creature can bear often or for long the full nearness of God's majesty in its beatitude…Yet there must still be such times, for they show the bright vision and completion of our sonship…though God indeed comes where and when He chooses, yet He will choose to come when we sincerely call upon Him and prepare ourselves truly for His visitation.[207]

A true revelation of God's glory, a visitation from the heavenly Fire, can light a spark in the darkest and most cold hearts and fulfill our deepest desire. Each day its flame will grow stronger, though after a while it may seem to wane. But the fire of Heaven will always return in the proper time, in the season when our hearts are most prepared.

Only a holy heart of worship can allow us to abide in the fire of the heavenly love. When we feel even the smallest portion of His glory, our cares, our fears, our anxieties, and our losses all melt away in that warm moment of divine affection, as our hearts rest in the rapture of His love.

We are trying to return Home to the Lord, and there is a mysterious bliss that awaits us each time we arrive. When we discover the proper highway we must travel, and learn to recognize the signs that indicate the road is near, we must make sure other things in our lives do not pull us off course and distract us from returning to the warmth of Home. We must travel the Way of Holiness, and do our best to stay on that blessed highway, because at home in His presence is where our hearts long to be, but "without holiness no one will see the Lord."[208]

"How lovely is your dwelling place, O LORD Almighty! My soul yearns, even faints, for the courts of the LORD; my heart and my flesh cry out for the living God. Even the sparrow has found a home, and the swallow a nest for herself, where she may have her young—a place near your altar, O LORD Almighty, my King and my God. Blessed are those who dwell in your house; they are ever praising you...Better is one day in your courts than a thousand elsewhere; I would rather be a doorkeeper in the house of my God than dwell in the tents of the wicked." Psalm 84:1-4, 10

-14-

PRECIOUS AND FINE PEARLS

THOUGHTS ON MAN'S EXCEEDINGLY GREAT REWARD
AND GOD'S PRICELESS POSSESSIONS

"The kingdom of heaven is like treasure hidden in a field. When a man found it, he hid it again, and then in his joy went and sold all he had and bought that field. Again, the kingdom of heaven is like a merchant looking for fine pearls. When he found one of great value, he went away and sold everything he had and bought it."
Matthew 13:44-46

The need for a chapter of this nature is no secret. The current mood of religious thinking in our country has, in large part, transformed the hand of God into the heart of God, the blessings of God into the fullness of God. I know only of the condition of much the Western Church and am not speaking for our brothers and sisters in Christ who have not lost the proper perspective of the kingdom. But certainly God blesses us, and we are definitely called to petition His hand when we are in need, and also when we are not in need, to receive His abundant and gracious blessings when He wills it.[209] Unfortunately, when our hearts wander away from the heart of the Father, our prayers turn hollow and selfish. Our religion certainly wanders from the purity of the one spoken of by James when he wrote about our spirituality saying, "Religion that God our Father accepts as pure and faultless...."

The sad truth about today is that "the world" that James warned us about has influenced our thinking and our religion. We are being polluted by unhealthy passions and selfish ambitions, and our purity is certainly beginning to wane.

"Religion of the heart" is slowly morphing into "religion of the want," as we consume the ideals the world has thrust upon us. In doing so, we are moving further and further away from the purity of a passion for the divine love and for the Kingdom of Heaven. As the degree of change within our hearts increases and we move away from the sanctified life of the cross, we are no longer the harbingers of love, but we pass on to the world an idea of God that is not fitting. We introduce them to a god who does not exist, and it is no wonder their prayers are not answered,[210] and not strange that their lives remain the same.

Our own evil desires direct our lives and our petitions to God; this shallow world, not transcendent love, is transforming our hearts and shaping our ambition. We have made ourselves God's enemies, because we have loved this sinful world. The enjoyment of the divine love is not our highest aim or our greatest blessing. We place value in simple and unholy things;

we envy earthly possessions and influence, but do not covet supernatural gain. Our mouths water at the thought of fame and fortune, but at the thoughts of God and His love—well, there is no room them.

The Christian life can suffer if its adherents are not vigilant in protecting their hearts against the trappings of the world. When the true God is removed from the throne of our lives and other pursuits become more valuable to us, a new god ascends in our hearts. This is our unsettling indication that we have begun to lose sight of the true splendor of a living relationship with God. No longer finding much worth in what is invisible and priceless we exchange our Glory for common aspirations and worthless treasures.

We all too often find ourselves in the unfortunate position of viewing His love and our relation to that love from a pitifully abhorrent perspective; as a result, He is profaned and displeased, and we are left unfulfilled. Our lives do not change, because we will not let God pour His love into us. Our hearts remain empty, because we filled it with vapor and not the waters of love divine.

Truthfully, it is only by God's gracious self-revelation that the any person is drawn toward their Creator and finds their self at the crossroads of a life-changing decision. On one road we can see the hand of God reaching out to us, and on the other, we see the world calling us to return to the simple freedom of our old, empty lives. Each person must choose which path to travel, and herein, we see how powerful and significant our thoughts about the things of God truly are. We must see our relationship with God as valuable, as something worth committing to, as something that deserves our sincere devotion. Otherwise, we cannot and we will not commit our hearts. Everything about our lives will adjust depending upon the way we approach the things of God, the value we place on having a personal experience with Him, and the concern we have for living a reverent life before Him.

It is no great mystery, then, why we have such a hard time committing to the way of love and defending our search for singular spiritual truth. Our perspective is feeble, so our commitment is little or non-existent. It does not seem valuable to us, so we are more prone to ignore it than we are to covet it. Because we do not covet it, we are not willing to part with anything to gain it. We see His love ingloriously, we do not honor Him "in the splendor of His holiness," and we shape our lives based on the perspective we hold.

Like the man with "great riches" who was not willing to part with his wealth to gain the glories of Heaven, it will be difficult for us to give up anything to experience the heart of the kingdom because, in our thinking, what we already have is too much to give up.[211] His wealth, in itself, was not wicked, but his inability to part with his riches showed that he loved his money and not the Lord of hearts. His perspective was unholy; He coveted his riches and could not realize how worthless his possessions truly were in comparison to what he was lacking in his soul and spirit.

When the nation of Israel was preparing to move into the land of promise, their inheritance was outlined so that each tribe would know which area would be designated as theirs. Likewise, we often look for God's material blessings and allotment as our sign of spiritual prosperity, forgetting that there was one tribe who did not receive a physical portion as the others did: to this tribe it was declared that *the Lord Himself* was their inheritance and their portion. Unfortunately, the command of Jesus, when He told His disciples, "remain in my love," goes unregarded and undervalued.[212] We do not see that there is no joy like the joy of abiding in Christ and in His love, making our home there, finding our allotment and our portion in Him, letting Him be our most coveted inheritance.

Material blessings and temporal rewards are only glimmers of the celestial and eternal blessing of the experience of God's presence and love in our lives. Through His gifts to us, we taste

His goodness and grace, but we should never allow ourselves to think, even for a moment, that they are God's most wonderful gifts to us.

Long ago, God told Abram, after promising him many wonderful blessings in life, that His nearness to His heart was his "exceedingly great reward."[213] Our mysterious Maker is the fullness of all our hopes, dreams, and desires. Enjoying His presence forever, is the reason for which we were made. If all we have is Christ, we have all we will ever need. The Lord is our true inheritance. He is our heart's greatest desire, and our soul's greatest reward. A spirit who has touched His love, who has been embraced by the arms of the invisible God in mysterious moments of joy, whose heart has felt the rush of the closeness of the Divine Presence in nights of sadness and pain, will know there is nothing else like it.

But I pray that one day, for both you and me, the words of the psalmist become true and living in our hearts. Asaph cried out to God, perhaps after being stirred in His heart by visions of glory and infinite love, saying "earth has nothing I desire besides you."[214] I will admit that the world has many enticing and entrapping lusts, anyone who has lived here for a good amount of time can confirm my findings, but the satisfaction of those vain pursuits is fleeting at best. Experience has, as it did to the curious King Solomon, taught me some valuable lessons.[215] The happiness that the pleasures of the world offer is only like the mist that appears for a little while and then vanishes. It has no substance that my heart can hold on to. Exciting and enticing they may be, for a time and for a season, but to me they are vanity.

They cannot fill the emptiness that life sometimes brings my way, when sad days and cold nights overwhelm me. This is the truth that I always find, whenever my heart chooses to stray from God: the world and its guilty pleasures are meaningless—it has no joy to speak of. God's presence is what my heart needs. He is my portion and the strength of my heart forever.

He is the one that gives me life; in fact, He is the True Life, and I found priceless joy that I will not give up for anything, by walking with the Divine Creator and worshipping His Son, Jesus Christ.

But like the lost little children we are, we often turn our hearts away toward new masters that we form out of our own conceit and ambition. We place those new idols on the loftiest mantles we have, and bow to them as if they can change our lives and bring us joy. We choose the road most often traveled, and instead of enjoying the quintessence of beauty and goodness we veer toward the mundane. We reject His revelation and truth, and do not find value in His gospel.

Nevertheless, while some of us might not find much value in God, rest assured, He places a particularly high value in our hearts. To God, we are something far more precious. To our Creator, those who long to know Him in love and adoration, in faith and truth, they are the hidden treasure of which Jesus spoke in His parable. The world is that field, and the faithful remnant is God's treasure. He looks for them, and hunts for them. Upon finding them, there is no price He will not pay to collect them for Himself, to keep them as His most treasured possession. He will horde them and gather them and keep them all to Himself. He will not share them with anything or anyone else; He wants them all to Himself. If anyone reaches to grab them from His hand, He will use His rod to rebuke that foolish thief, for they are His, and He will not share them.

Then He will look down at His priceless possession, we who are in His hand forever,[216] and He will say to us what He has always longed to tell us, "I have loved you with an everlasting love; I have drawn you with loving-kindness…Never will I leave you; never will I forsake you…You are my people."

But if we could gain a better perspective, rather, a proper perspective in the way in which we view the beauty of our God, I am sure our lives would be far different. I dare say that we were created *because* of a love that cannot be properly defined or totally understood; created *for* a love that words and reason cannot picture or comprehend. The human experience, then, is definitively about love, that is, a relationship with the Source of all goodness and the true devotion that He desires.

Yet, when we begin to place anything else in this world above it, we err. When we lose sight of the Divine One's true beauty, the supreme experience of life is then packaged away in obscurity, stored in a small box in a large warehouse that no one ever visits. The goal of creation is dishonored, and our greatest gift is lost.

The divine love is the reflection of the nature of the God we are called to follow in adoration and to run after in desire. It is the fiery passion that burns for His created children, it is certainly that which we were created to enjoy, and although it is not what we are called to worship, it inspires it nonetheless.

It is our true abode, a place where we can rest after a long day traveling in the heat, a home where love is. No wonder Jesus told His disciples to remain in His love. He wanted them to live there and to make their home within. This is why the old teacher said:

> Our abode, the home of our soul, is to be the love of Christ. We are to live our life there, to be at home there all the day…[Remaining] Abiding means going out from everything else to occupy one place and stay there. Come away from all else, set your heart on Jesus and His love, and that love will waken your faith and strengthen it…You may be sure it will reach out to you, and by its power take you up into itself as your abode and your home.[217]

This is eternal life. This is our place of rest: abiding in the love of Christ. Swimming in the depths of that great mystery and enjoying all the beauty it has to offer, finding relief from the burning heat of loneliness, in the waters of our divine Companion. The late mystic's words are blessed: "Eternal Life is that 'blessed vision wherewith the Infinite God looketh into the deep of a man's soul; and in so looking vivifieth it by a communication of love."[218]

This is "the hope of glory" mentioned in Paul's letter to the Colossians: to be united with God in love, through the indwelling presence of Jesus Christ in our hearts, and sealed with the promise of everlasting and unending spiritual bliss by the precious Holy Spirit.[219]

If there must be a closing chapter to my current collection of thoughts, I think it is fitting that this would be that chapter. In the most spiritual sense possible, *A Collection of Thoughts on the Mystery of Love* can never be complete. There will always be more majesty and beauty for us to enjoy and to explore on the mysterious waters of the Divine. We can all have our own collection of thoughts on the mystery of love, and I am sure that immediately upon observing the title of this work, your minds had already begun the task of compiling your own personal manifesto. The true test, however, is whether or not those thoughts you compile reflect the reality of what we can know to be true about the mystery of divine love and about the nature of the God who is the essence of that love. Although one day someone might be bold enough to say, "I have the answer, I have deciphered the mystery!" we know that he is at best a fool, and at worst a liar.

We should be thankful that we cannot know everything about His love or His nature. I think, from a proper perspective, He would not seem as special if we could. If God could be known completely, He would then cease to be God. If we could know His love, without some shade of mystery still remaining, it could not possibly be worth our commitment and awe, for it would cease to be the emanation of the character of an eternal and transcendent God.

When we truly taste God's glory and observe His splendor, then our perspective changes, then we will give up all we have to attain that great treasure that is the knowledge of God and the satisfaction of His love. Then it will be worth our time, our commitment, and our hearts. Until then, the idea of God's love for His children is simply an afterthought to the world at large. It is merely a motto of commercial religion and philosophy, a banner of churches large and small, a luring tool of cults and exploiters, a friendly aphorism that people share in greetings and farewells, but one that carries with it no true, spiritual life; an idea and a word that has no great impact in our hearts.

That being said, I am encouraged because I know that in the hearts and the lives of a faithful few the fire of God's love will never be extinguished. The glow of Heaven will never be lost. It may be ignored, but the divine fire will never be quenched. Churches may one day grow smaller and smaller, and the world's evils may grow tremendously, but I know that God's love for us will remain forever.

As always, in the hearts and the lives of a faithful few, it will shine like the light of day. The world may grow darker still, but His light will shine brighter. I pay no mind to statistics that point out whether this or that religion is growing and dwarfing Christianity. Nor do figures about young people or disillusioned people abandoning the faith strike me as strange or disheartening in the least. It is sad to hear about people turning away from Jesus, and it is God's hope that all souls would come to know Him, but the words of His beloved Son foretold these issues long ago: "small is the gate and narrow the road that leads to [eternal] life, and only a few find it."[220]

Be that as it may, God is not concerned with size; He might very well prefer the greater numbers, but we can be sure He is satisfied with a few hearts that hunger and thirst for Him alone. A few souls that longed for truth, who refused to exchange their Glory. I know His love and power are real, others know the same, and we will persevere until we are called home to Heaven. We will spread our message of faith, hope, and love knowing that the road we are traveling is narrow and not wide. We are a special and peculiar people, and numbers too big might make our experience seem far too common to be supernal, thus diluting the preciousness and the holiness of our experience. Those who found that narrow road know that God's heart has substance. They know that God's love for His children is the great hope of a living spirituality. And they know that God's presence is an active reality in the hearts of those who believe.

As it is, there may be hundreds of millions of self-professed Christians in the world today, but the number of the true faithful, we can be sure, is much smaller, and in that fact we are sanctified by God. The number of those who have met with God in personal experience, who have discovered the gloriousness of His manifest presence, and who have irrefutable knowledge of His goodness that cannot be stolen from them is small—this I know.[221]

I hope that as you have read my collection of thoughts on the mystery of love, some of my thoughts might have become yours also, and that those thoughts of the Holy One might move you toward a higher realm of contemplation—one where you never forget the holy and heavenly passion that burns for you. "Herein truly is perfect love; when all the intent of the mind, all the secret working of the heart, is lifted up into the love of God."[222]

I am convinced that the answer to every problem of the human experience can be found in the heart of God. So, like many other faithful ones before us, we must dedicate our hearts and our lives to the pursuit of this most blessed experience. We must lift our thoughts to the heavens to gain a proper perspective on the mystery of love. Then revelation will open our eyes and we will finally see things clearly. We will know that abiding in the heart of our Creator and enjoying His love forever is the supreme experience of the human existence. We will realize that we are spiritual creatures, who will only be satisfied as we enjoy a spiritual love. We will understand that we are valuable to God, far more valuable than we can ever know.

The number of the true faithful may be very small, but that

makes us unique and rare creatures. He looks at each one of our hearts and smiles as a father smiles over his newborn child. He covets our affection as a man covets a treasure, and He holds us close to His heart. Without a doubt, God's people are His most priceless possession, and He will not give them up for anything. He will defend that treasure with all His power, so that no one can snatch them from His hand. To God, their hearts are valuable; they are like precious and fine pearls.

"On one occasion an expert in the law stood up to test Jesus. 'Teacher,' he asked, 'what must I do to inherit eternal life?' 'What is written in the Law?' he replied. 'How do you read it?' He answered: 'Love the Lord your God with all your heart and with all your soul and with all your strength and with all your mind'; and, 'Love your neighbor as yourself.' 'You have answered correctly,' Jesus replied. 'Do this and you will live.'" Luke 10:25-28

ENDNOTES

Preface

[1] 2 Timothy 2:13
[2] Gonzalez C.G. & Gonzalez J.L. (2008). *Heretics for Armchair Theologians*, p.78
[3] Ibid.
[4] Romans 1:20
[5] Murray, A. (2007). *The True Vine*, p.23
[6] Erdman, C.R. (1950). *The Book of Genesis*, p.15
[7] Genesis 1:27
[8] Genesis 2:7
[9] Revelation 4:11
[10] John 17:3
[11] Ephesians 3:19
[12] Matthew 25:14-30
[13] Tozer, A.W. (1998). *The Knowledge of the Holy*, p.98

Chapter 1: "The End of Desire"

[14] 1 John 4:7
[15] Isaiah 55:1a
[16] Psalm 107:4-5
[17] Luke 6:21
[18] James 1:14-16, (emphasis mine)
[19] Ephesians 4:18-19
[20] Hebrews 11:6
[21] Revelation 3:20
[22] Psalm 108:3-4
[23] Romans 1:20
[24] Robertson, F.W. Excerpt from "Jacob's Wrestling." (*Ten Sermons*) June 10, 1849
[25] Genesis 41:48-49
[26] Tozer, A.W. (2007). *The Pursuit of God*
[27] Cusa, N.O. (2007). *The Vision of God*, p.76-77

Chapter 2: "They Shall See God"

[28] Titus 1:15-16
[29] Jeremiah 4:14
[30] Genesis 6:5-6
[31] Proverbs 15:26
[32] Mark 7:20-23
[33] Romans 1:18-22
[34] Psalm 50:21
[35] Habakkuk 1:13
[36] Matthew 5:8

Chapter 3: "Deep and Hidden Things"

[37] Deuteronomy 6:4-9
[38] Colossians 1:16-17
[39] Hebrews 11
[40] Job 11:7-9
[41] Proverbs 2:3-5
[42] Psalm 97:2a
[43] Daniel 2:28

[44] Daniel 2:21-22
[45] Proverbs 2:6
[46] Deuteronomy 29:29, 1 Corinthians 4:1
[47] Hebrews 11:6
[48] 1 Timothy 4:16
[49] Psalm 119:105
[50] Romans 1:19
[51] Daniel 2:21-22

Chapter 4: "A Horrible Misunderstanding"

[52] John 13:34-35
[53] Matthew 5:1-16
[54] Matthew 5
[55] Tozer, A.W. (2009). *Reclaiming Christianity: A Call to Authentic Faith*, p.109
[56] 1 John 4
[57] Hebrews 7:26, (emphasis mine)
[58] Hebrews 1:3
[59] 2 Chronicles 20:21, (emphasis mine).
[60] Ezekiel 22:25-29, (emphasis mine)
[61] Matthew 5:9
[62] Psalm 111:10, Proverbs 1:7, Proverbs 9:10
[63] 2 Peter 1:4
[64] 1 Corinthians 13:1-8a

Chapter 5: "His Treasured Possession"

[65] Tozer, A.W. (1998). *The Knowledge of the Holy*, p.1
[66] Matthew 7:6
[67] Proverbs 1:7
[68] Malachi 3:16-18
[69] Hosea 4:6-7, Romans 1:18-32
[70] Romans 1:19
[71] 1 Corinthians 2:14
[72] Ephesians 3:16-19
[73] 1 Corinthians 2:10-12, (emphasis mine)
[74] Colossians 3:1
[75] Aquinas, T. (1999). *Aquinas: Selected Writings*, p.521
[76] Matthew 16:13-17
[77] Hosea 4, Jeremiah 2

Chapter 6: "The Light was Good"

[78] Isaiah 9:2
[79] Job 10:21-22
[80] John 3:19-20
[81] John 12:46
[82] Isaiah 60:1-2

Chapter 7: "Trustworthy and True"

[83] Proverbs 20:6
[84] Hebrews 11:1-2
[85] John 15:1-17
[86] Murray, A. (2007). *The True Vine*, p.79-80
[87] Proverbs 3:5

[88] James 4:13-16
[89] Proverbs 16:9
[90] Psalm 9:10
[91] Ephesians 1:3
[92] Exodus 3:1-15
[93] Sumrall, L. (1993). *The Names of God: God's Character Revealed Through His Names*, p.8
[94] James 1:17
[95] Psalm 89:2
[96] Revelation 3:14, 19:11, 21:5

Chapter 8: "My People"

[97] Proverbs 27:12
[98] 1 Timothy 6
[99] 1 Samuel 15
[100] Genesis 2-3
[101] 2 Timothy 4:3
[102] (2007). *The Apologetics Study Bible,* Article by William Lane Craig, "What About Those Who Have Never Heard of Christ?" p.1696
[103] Romans 1
[104] (2003). *Webster's Dictionary for Students*, p.331, summary of "religion" and "religious"
[105] Ephesians 2:22
[106] James 1:27
[107] Murray, A. (2007). *The True Vine*, p.113
[108] Isaiah 1:16-17
[109] Lewis, C.S. (2005) *What Christians Believe*, p.3-4
[110] Revelation 21-22
[111] Galatians 5
[112] Murray, A. (1984). *The Believer's Full Blessing of Pentecost*, p.74
[113] Colossians 1:15-20
[114] Excerpt from "Nonviolence and Racial Justice," Martin Luther King, Jr.
[115] John 14-16, Romans 5:5
[116] (2007). *The Apologetics Study Bible,* Article by Ted Cabal, "Notable Christian Apologist: Justin Martyr," p.1900
[117] Psalm 24:1
[118] Matthew 4:17
[119] Genesis 14:18-20
[120] See the story "Pandora's Box" and Genesis Chapters 2-3
[121] 1 Timothy 2:4
[122] Matthew 15:14
[123] James 1:25
[124] Jude 1:4, (emphasis mine)
[125] John 14:6, (emphasis mine)
[126] Psalm 24:3-5
[127] Isaiah 51
[128] Luke 13:34
[129] Romans 1
[130] Jeremiah 31:6
[131] Tozer, A.W. (1998). *The Knowledge of the Holy*, p.vii
[132] Isaiah 51:15-16

Chapter 9: "All Things Exist for Him"

[133] Psalm 19:1
[134] Psalm 33:6,9
[135] Psalm 1:6

[136] Which means "man"
[137] Philippians 4:5
[138] Psalm 10:4
[139] Acts 17:24-25
[140] Numbers 21:4-8
[141] John 6:40
[142] Hall, C. & Redman, M. (2005). "Center"
[143] Romans 11:36
[144] John 10:10b
[145] Nicholi Jr., A.M. (2003). *The Question of God*, p.206
[146] Tozer, A.W. (2009). *Reclaiming Christianity: A Call to Authentic Faith*, p.185
[147] Isaiah 55:6
[148] Murray, A. (2007). *The True Vine*, p.83
[149] Hebrews 2:10

Chapter 10: "I Was Not Aware"

[150] Jeremiah 31:3
[151] John 10:3-5
[152] Cusa, N.O. (2007). *The Vision of God*, p.3-6
[153] Ibid, p.41-42
[154] John 3:16, (emphasis mine)
[155] Romans 5:8, (emphasis mine)
[156] 2 Chronicles 2:6
[157] Tozer, A.W. (1998). *The Knowledge of the Holy*, p.76
[158] Psalm 139:1-3
[159] Exodus 19
[160] Hebrews 10:22
[161] Luke 13, Revelation 3:19, Ezekiel 18:31-32
[162] Acts 17:26-27
[163] Psalm 139:7-12
[164] 1 John 4:7-18
[165] Genesis 28:16

Chapter 11: "Your Voice is Sweet"

[166] Isaiah 6
[167] Psalm 29:4
[168] John 5:25
[169] Deuteronomy 8:3, Matthew 4:4
[170] Hebrews 1:3
[171] 1 Peter 3:12
[172] John 17:13-17
[173] Romans 4:17
[174] Genesis 1:1-3
[175] Revelation 4:11
[176] Psalm 33:6-9
[177] Matthew 13:13,15
[178] Deuteronomy 5:23-25
[179] Daniel 3
[180] Daniel 3
[181] Hebrews 4:7
[182] Hebrews 3:12-15
[183] Revelation 3:20
[184] John 10:4,27
[185] Song of Solomon 2:14

Chapter 12: "Because I am Holy"

[186] Hebrews 11:6, (emphasis mine)
[187] Isaiah 64:6a
[188] Romans 7:24
[189] Habakkuk 1:13
[190] Psalm 10:11
[191] Isaiah 53
[192] (2004). *Nelson's Compact Series: Compact Bible Dictionary*, p.250, "Grace"
[193] Numbers 6:24-26
[194] Proverbs 3:34
[195] Ephesians 2:3-9, (emphasis mine)
[196] 1 Peter 1:13-16

Chapter 13: "No One Will See the Lord"

[197] John 4:23
[198] 2 Samuel 6
[199] John 8:32
[200] Suso, *German Writings*, ed. Denifle, p.289
[201] Isaiah 35:8-10
[202] Romans 12:1
[203] 2 Corinthians 7:1
[204] Ibid.
[205] Romans 8:1
[206] Otto, R. (1958). *The Idea of the Holy*, p.211
[207] Ibid, p.214
[208] Hebrews 12:14

Chapter 14: "Precious and Fine Pearls"

[209] Ephesians 6:18
[210] James 4:3-5
[211] Matthew 19:16-30
[212] John 15:1-17
[213] Genesis 15:1
[214] Psalm 73:25
[215] Ecclesiastes
[216] Hebrews 13:5
[217] Murray, A. (2007). *The True Vine*, p.99-101
[218] Cusa, N.O. (2007). *The Vision of God*, p. xiii
[219] Colossians 1:25-27
[220] Matthew 7:13-14
[221] Deuteronomy 7:6-9
[222] Rolle, R. (1927). *The Amending of Life*, p.83-84

www.ingramcontent.com/pod-product-compliance
Lightning Source LLC
Chambersburg PA
CBHW032119090426
42743CB00007B/394